PhilanthropyRoundtable

From Promising to Proven

A Wise Giver's Guide to Expanding on the Success of Charter Schools

Karl Zinsmeister

Research assistance by Public Impact
Karl Zinsmeister, series editor

Published by The Philanthropy Roundtable, 1730 M Street NW, Suite 601, Washington, DC, 20036.

Free copies of this book are available to qualified donors. To learn more, or to order more copies, call (202) 822-8333, e-mail main@PhilanthropyRoundtable.org, or visit PhilanthropyRoundtable.org. An e-book version is available from major online booksellers. A PDF may be downloaded at no charge at PhilanthropyRoundtable.org.

Cover: © Studio-Pro / istockphoto

ISBN 978-0-9892202-3-1
LCCN 2014933932

First printing, March 2014

Current and Upcoming
Wise Giver's Guides from
The Philanthropy Roundtable

Karl Zinsmeister, *series editor*

For all current and future titles, visit PhilanthropyRoundtable.org/guidebook

TABLE OF CONTENTS

PREFACE

Charter Schools Are Taking Off

When you ask America's most seasoned and effective K-12 education givers which philanthropic investments have been most transformative over the last generation, charter schools rank at or near the top. For all of the inconsistency that exists within the sector, it has proven to be the laboratory, workhorse, and guiding light of K-12 education. Thousands of charter schools around the nation offer dramatically better options than students would otherwise receive. This is especially true for students from lower-income neighborhoods.

Charters are expanding rapidly. For the sector to live up to its creed—autonomy to develop schools that perform better than traditional options, in exchange for accountability for results—philanthropists must make quality the watchword. Charter schooling is not without its failures and pitfalls. Philanthropists investing in charters must give in a wise and informed way.

Donors large and small, many profiled in this guidebook, have shown that philanthropy can fuel sustained charter school growth. The most sophisticated use their giving to also undergird excellence and shape public policy to promote innovation, autonomy, and accountability. The flowering of charter schools has been led by philanthropy, and donors must continue in their leading role if today's millions of children still unable to access a quality education are to gain a better option. Exciting work remains.

The Philanthropy Roundtable gratefully acknowledges the generous support of the Laura and John Arnold Foundation and Mrs. Donald G. Fisher toward the publication of this guidebook.

Whatever your funding priorities, if you would like to enter a network of hundreds of top donors from across the country who share lessons learned and debate future strategies, we hope you will consider joining The Philanthropy Roundtable. We offer intellectually challenging and solicitation-free meetings, customized resources, consulting, and private seminars for our members, all at no charge.

For more information, please feel free to contact any of us at K-12@PhilanthropyRoundtable.org or (202) 822-8333.

Adam Meyerson, president, The Philanthropy Roundtable
Dan Fishman, director of K–12 education programs
Anthony Pienta, deputy director of K–12 education programs

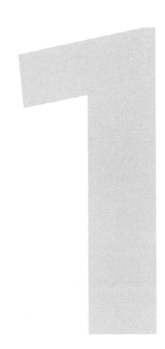

A Breakthrough Decade for Charter Schools

For years, philanthropists large and small have labored to improve student outcomes at ineffective public schools. From the Ford Foundation's decades of interventions, to hordes of concerned corporate donors hoping to encourage excellence, to the $1.1 billion spent as a result of Walter Annenberg's philanthropic challenge, these donors ended up with shockingly little to show for their large efforts.

Then in 1991, Minnesota pioneered the concept of public schools operated by nonprofits or other independent parties. Teachers and leaders in these schools were given great autonomy, but faced closure if the school didn't show good student results. California passed a similiar law the next year. The first charter school opened in 1992.

Beginning from nothing, the charter school movement took root slowly. At year ten, the total number of American children in charters passed half a million. And donors began to notice some startling patterns.

Bill Gates explains that after his foundation decided in the mid-1990s to focus on U.S. schooling, it poured about $2 billion into various education experiments. During their first decade, he reports, "many of the small schools that we invested in did not improve students' achievement in any significant way." There was, however, one fascinating exception. "A few of the schools that we funded achieved something amazing. They replaced schools with low expectations and low results with ones that have high expectations and high results." And there was a common variable: "Almost all of these schools were charter schools."

Other philanthropists had the same experience. Eli Broad, one of the biggest givers to education in the U.S., observed that "charter school systems are delivering the best student outcomes, particularly for poor and minority students. They are performing significantly better than the best traditional school district systems." Ted Mitchell of the NewSchools Venture Fund drew some bold bottom lines: "Good charter schools have pretty much eliminated the high-school dropout rate. And they've doubled the college-going rate of underserved kids."

In recent years, the number, variety, and quality of charter schools started to soar. By 2014 there were 2.6 million children attending 6,500 charter schools in the U.S. Every year now, more than 600 new charters open their doors for the first time, and an additional 300,000 children enroll (while a million kids remain on waiting lists, with millions more hungrily waiting in the wings). Charter school attendance began to particularly accelerate around 2009, and as this is written in 2014 it looks like there may be 5 million children in charters before the end of the decade.

There are great charter schools and poor charter schools, and the charter sector as a whole has weaknesses as well as strengths. We'll examine these problems in this book. The charter boom, though, is only going to get bigger. All but eight states are now experimenting with charters. Already, one out of every 19 American schoolchildren is enrolled in a charter school, and by five years from now that is likely to double to one out of every nine.

There is an argument to be made that charter schooling is the most important social innovation in America of the past generation. And it bubbled up spontaneously from our grassroots, without much establishment support. To its very marrow, it is a product of independent social entrepreneurs and private philanthropy.

What's distinctive about charter schools?
First let's get some general facts on the table.

What are charter schools?
- Public schools, funded with public money
- Privately managed (by organizations "chartered" by a public authority)
- Must meet the same graduation requirements as other schools
- Open to all, and tuition-free for every student
- Often aided by philanthropy (because public funding for operations averages only four fifths of the level enjoyed by other public schools, and facilities are often not funded in any way)
- Have no claim to neighborhood students; families must choose the school
- Select students randomly by lottery when applicants exceed available slots
- Operate autonomously, free of many of the conventions and union rules that district schools follow
- Can be a stand-alone school, or part of a network of charter schools; can be nonprofit or for-profit
- Frequently specialize to meet the needs of targeted students (dropouts, math achievers, artists, English-language learners, etc.)
- Two thirds of existing charter students are minorities; approximately the same proportion are low-income
- Charter schools are subject to closure if they fail to improve student achievement

More consequential innovations in educational practice have bubbled up out of charter schools over the past two decades than from the rest of our K-12 schools combined. Following are some areas where charters have led the way.

- Longer school days
- Longer school years
- Higher expectations for students (e.g. 100 percent college acceptance at many leading inner-city charters)
- Recruitment of excellent teachers outside of traditional credential channels
- Linking compensation to student results, yielding better pay for more effective teachers
- Stricter discipline; more structured school day
- Asking parents and students to sign contracts that commit them to serious duties that parallel the school's efforts to teach
- Experiments with advancement by demonstrated competency in a subject, rather than rigid age or grade levels
- Curricular invention—like blended learning and other technology leaps, more AP classes, Core Knowledge instruction, special science and engineering programs, etc.
- More rigorous testing that is shared with parents, regulators, and public to aid assessment of school quality (including standardized tests, PISA tests, and the highly personalized testing at the heart of blended learning)

Some broad strengths of charter schools

- They attract more entrepreneurial principals and teachers into the field of education
- School autonomy allows wide experimentation with new ways of educating
- This same flexibility is used to circumvent bureaucratic obstacles that often block conventional schools from succeeding
- Charters sidestep the dysfunctional labor relations of many urban districts
- They erode monopolies and introduce competitive energy into public education
- Research shows that charters are more effective at recruiting teachers who graduated in the top third of their college class
- Charters give parents who cannot afford private schools, or moving, another choice besides their neighborhood school
- They give nonprofits and community organizations practical opportunities to improve the education of local children

- Their emphasis on student outcomes fosters greater accountability for results
- By functioning as laboratories and alternatives, charters foment change in conventional schools as well

The structural strengths of charter schools can cumulate to produce dramatic successes. In the 2013 *U.S. News and World Report* rankings of public high schools, for instance, 41 charters made it into the top 200. Given that charter schools represent about 5 percent of the high-school market, a finding that 21 percent of our best institutions are charters is an impressive over-representation.

Perhaps even more impressive is the repeatedly demonstrated ability of top charter schools to take cohorts of students that are 80 or 90 percent disadvantaged and turn far-above-average proportions of them into high-school graduates, college students, and successful adults. Here are a few snapshots pulled from a very long movie reel of successes:

- The 9,000 students at Uncommon Schools are 78 percent low-income and 98 percent African-American or Hispanic, yet all seniors take the SAT, and their average score is 20 points above the college-readiness benchmark
- At KIPP charter schools, home to 51,000 pupils in 21 states, 96 percent of eighth graders perform better than their local district counterparts on reading, and 92 percent perform better in math
- Among charter school students in Washington, D.C. (almost half of that city's public school population), the on-time high-school graduation rate is 21 percentage points higher than that among conventional school students: 77 percent to 56 percent
- In New Orleans—long an educational disaster zone—the city schools rank first in the state for student growth now that more than eight out of ten students attend charters (some details on the Big Easy's charter experience will follow in just a few pages)

Reaching critical mass?
With the promise they have shown, it's no surprise that the audience for charter schools should have mushroomed the way it has in recent years.

U.S. students in charter schools

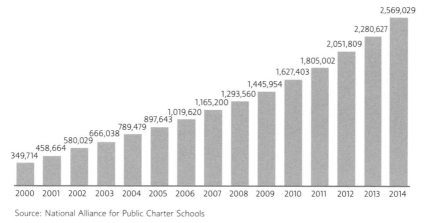

Source: National Alliance for Public Charter Schools

This growth has not been at all geographically even. There are many places the charter school revolution has not yet touched, and other places that are hotspots. California is the state with more charter schools than any other—1,130 schools that are educating 8 percent of all the state's schoolchildren. On a percentage basis, the most advanced state is Arizona, where one out of every six kids is enrolled in a charter (605 schools).

Here are the states leading the charter parade:

State	# of campuses	% of students in charters
Arizona	605	16%
Colorado	197	10
Florida	625	9
Michigan	297	9
California	1,130	8
Ohio	400	7
Hawaii	33	6
Texas	689	5
Wisconsin	245	5
New York	233	4

Source: National Alliance for Public Charter Schools, author extrapolations for latest year.

The fraction of all children attending charters rises even higher in particular metro areas. These are the cities where charter schools currently have the highest market share:

City	% of students in charters
New Orleans	84%
Detroit	51
Washington, D.C.	43
Flint, Michigan	36
Kansas City, Missouri	35
Gary, Indiana	35
Gainesville, Georgia	32
Cleveland	29
Indianapolis	28
Philadelphia	27
Dayton, Ohio	27
Albany, New York	26
Phoenix	26
Toledo, Ohio	26
San Antonio	26
Grand Rapids, Michigan	25

Source: National Alliance for Public Charter Schools

Some other metro areas where charter schools have built up momentum in one way or another include Houston, Los Angeles, Miami, Atlanta, Memphis, New York City, Boston, Milwaukee, St. Louis, Chicago, and Minneapolis.

Close-up on Houston

Two cities where charter schools have flowered thanks to massive philanthropic outpourings are Houston and New Orleans. We'll briefly consider each of their cases.

As the nation's seventh largest school district, Houston has been plagued with the familiar problems of urban public education. A 2009 study found that only 59 percent of youngsters starting ninth grade in the Houston school district will have graduated from high school six years later. (It adjusted for students who leave the system, which the district's official statistics ignore.)

Just about the time that that research was being concluded, local and national donors were plotting an attack on Houston's educational underachievement. Two of the most effective charter networks in the U.S.—KIPP and YES Prep—were born in Houston. So it is appropriate that they are now leading the city toward a new charter-inspired educational structure, via a massive, rapid expansion of their respective school chains across the city. KIPP and YES agreed to launch more than 50 new campuses and open up tens of thousands of additional seats where pupils previously languishing in ineffective district schools could get a fresh chance at learning. Philanthropists put more than $90 million behind their efforts.

The intent was not only to boost the families using these schools, but also to spark improvements in the wider school district, and set an example of bold citywide reform. "We will have many more students in a successful model that is working beside the district school system," summarized donor Jeff Hines. "Will that inspire the monopoly that has been in place to raise their game a bit?"

The Hines family and four other donors offered up eight-figure gifts to the Houston experiment:

Donors	Amount
Houston Endowment	$20 million
Michael & Susan Dell Foundation	$11 million
Jeff and Wendy Hines	$10 million
John and Laura Arnold	$10 million
Bill & Melinda Gates Foundation	$10 million

Many other Houstonians also gave generously: Jan and Dan Duncan ($4 million), the Brown Foundation ($6 million), Tony Annunziato ($2 million), the Fondren Foundation ($1 million), Jim McIngvale ($1 million), the George Foundation ($1 million), the Rockwell Fund ($1 million) and others. From out of town, education super-donors Donald & Doris Fisher chipped in more than $5 million, the Amy and Larry Robbins Foundation contributed $2 million, the Charter School Growth Fund put up $2 million, and the Walton Family Foundation pledged $9 million. An important adviser to the effort was Leo Linbeck III, a Houston businessman and philanthropist and expert in rapidly growing firms, who provided much of the planning.

As of the 2014 writing of this book, the Houston KIPP and YES school expansions are roughly half complete. KIPP now totals 22 schools and more than 10,000 pupils in the city, on the way to its goal of 42 schools and 21,000 students. YES Prep has reached 13 schools and 8,000 students, heading for an eventual Houston enrollment of 17,000.

Thanks in considerable degree to the rapid growth of these two providers, one out of every five schoolchildren in Houston is already attending a charter school. (That's more than 45,000 pupils in charters.) The proportion will rise much higher as KIPP and YES create an additional 20,000 seats, while other charter operators undertake their own expansions.

And with KIPP and YES known for producing extraordinary results with underprivileged kids, many of Houston's charters are of a high quality. The standardized test scores of YES Prep's heavily low-income and nearly all minority students, for instance, are consistently higher in every subject than the average score across Texas. Their dropout rate of 1 percent compares to 16 percent in the Houston public-school district.

Close-up on New Orleans

During the same period when Houston was gearing up its charter sector, New Orleans was stirring up a social hurricane of its own. With our current decade of hindsight, one may conclude that the biggest positive to come out of the destruction wrought by Katrina has been the complete remake of the dreadful New Orleans public schools. The city didn't just pour new wine into old bottles. Educators at the local, state, and national level pushed the reset button and dedicated themselves to creating an entirely different system that would not only brighten the life prospects of area children but also inspire and inform brave school reforms in other places.

Before the hurricane, New Orleans was the poorest-performing school district in the second-lowest-scoring state for K–12 education. Fully 78 percent of NOLA students attended a school designated as "failing" by state standards. Then the storm completely wrecked 100 of the district's 127 schools. Students were unable to even attend classes for six months.

At that point a group of leaders coalesced and decided that the schools should be rebuilt in an all-new "Recovery School District" that would largely be a necklace of independent charter schools strung together to pursue higher common standards. Decision-making power was decentralized away from the pre-storm school board bureaucracy, and transferred to individual school principals, teachers, and charter school boards. School performance began to be intensely monitored, with the understanding that the new schools granted five-year operating charters would be closed down at the end of that period if their students were not succeeding. Parents of public-school students gained unprecedented choice and options, which allow them to enroll their children in almost any school in the district.

This was bold new territory never before explored on a large scale in any city. It required creative thinking, canny strategy, and a high tolerance for risk. Those are scarce commodities within government bureaucracies, and it is certain that without the intense mobilization organized by philanthropists, the New Orleans experiment would never have borne fruit.

There has been a huge surge of donated money, expertise, and volunteer labor into New Orleans. Major philanthropic investors have included the Laura and John Arnold Foundation, Walton Family Foundation, Eli and

New Orleans became the first city in America where the majority of students attend charters, and there have already been stark improvements in student learning.

Edythe Broad Foundation, Bill & Melinda Gates Foundation, W. K. Kellogg Foundation, Carnegie Corporation, Fisher Fund, Robertson Foundation, and Louis Calder Foundation. Important local donors have included the Patrick Taylor Foundation, Booth-Bricker Fund, RosaMary Foundation, Baptist Community Ministries, Entergy, Capital One, and Chase.

These funders refused to simply write checks to established organizations. They set up crucial new oversight and assistance organizations like New Schools for New Orleans. They helped local social entrepreneurs plan and build new charter schools. They spent lots of money bolstering efforts by groups like Teach for America and TNTP to draw talented instructors and administrators to the city. Recently, there has been a concerted push by donors to attract some of the most successful charter operators from other parts of the country.

It is estimated that philanthropists have been pouring about $20 million per year into New Orleans charter schooling. While that represents only a fraction of the city's total spending on education, this seed capital has been carefully focused on the crucial levers of reform. As a result, it has been highly effective in moving the local education sector away from business as usual and in a dramatically new direction.

New Orleans quickly became the first city in America where the majority of public school students were attending charter schools. By the 2012-2013 school year, 84 percent of all local school kids were in charters. And already there have been stark improvements in student learning.

The fraction of public school students in New Orleans attended a school designated as "failing" was cut in half in the first few years; it is expected to be reduced to fewer than 5 percent by 2016. Every year, the students in New Orleans's charter schools post the highest performance growth in the state. The percentage of students achieving at or above their appropriate grade level increased 25 percent from 2007 to 2011.

> This transformation of the New Orleans educational system may turn out to be the most significant national development in education since desegregation.

NOLA students reaching or exceeding "Basic" proficiency on state tests jumped from 35 to 63 percent between 2005 and 2013. The high-school dropout rate is now half what it was in 2005.

In 2013, the Center for Research on Education Outcomes at Stanford University released in-depth findings that tracked results in New Orleans from 2006 to 2011. The study compared New Orleans students in charters versus conventional schools and found that in a given school year, the typical charter student made five months of extra progress in math and four months of extra learning in reading.

The CEO of New Schools for New Orleans, Neerav Kingsland, recently noted that "since 2006 New Orleans students have halved the achievement gap with their state counterparts. In the next five years, New Orleans will likely be the first urban city in the country to surpass its state average." Kingsland suggests that "this transformation of the New Orleans educational system may turn out to be the most significant national development in education since desegregation."

One should not exaggerate the state of the schools in New Orleans; they started in America's K-12 basement, and they've so far only climbed up to the ground floor. The chief schools officer at New Schools for New Orleans, Maggie Runyan-Shefa, says bluntly that "college readiness is the goal, and where the typical student in Louisiana is right now is not college ready. We are excited by what New Orleans has been able to do. It didn't take a generation. It didn't take decades. It took five to six years. But we are nowhere near where we want to be."

Her colleague Kingsland agrees. "Since Katrina, philanthropically driven charter schooling has helped us move from 'F' to 'C.' In the years ahead, it will be vital as we progress from 'C' to 'A.'"

Going from C to A: Crummy charters cannot be ignored

The past decade proved that charter schools can really shine. In the decade to come, an important project for philanthropists and authorizers will be to improve or close down the ineffective charters that sometimes share a city with good and great charters. That simply cannot be avoided if the overall grade for charter schooling is to be pulled up from "C" or "B" to a clear shining "A."

It isn't just in New Orleans that the composite result from all charter schools isn't yet where it needs to be. If you visit lots of K-12 campuses today, you'll find that in a given city the best institutions almost always include several charters. Unfortunately it is not uncommon to also find some charters among the worst performers. As is perhaps not surprising for such a new and inherently experimental, risk-taking social invention, the quality of charter schools is uneven.

A 2011 study looked at performance data from 720 charters in California, to see how many performed among the top 5 percent of all schools in the state versus the bottom 5 percent. The results showed that charters vary a lot more than conventional schools—more highs, more lows, less middling. As a group, charters were likelier to be very good than very bad: 16.0 percent fell in the top bracket, 11.5 percent in the bottom bracket. Compared to conventional schools, charters were 4.1 times likelier to be stars, and 2.6 times likelier to be goats.

The idea that good charters and bad charters are equally common, and thus chartering on the whole is of no help, is out of date and inaccurate. The continued existence of poor charters, however, underlines the importance of fixing or closing them (a subject we'll examine in detail in Chapter 3). The overall performance of charters on behalf of children and families will zip upward once the laggards have been lopped off.

The definitive research on this subject has been done by Stanford's Center for Research on Education Outcomes (CREDO). For some years now they have been collecting data from schools in 27 states that enroll 95 percent of U.S. charter students. The CREDO researchers zero in on hard measures of achievement (primarily test scores), make adjustments for demographic and economic status of the students being compared, and provide comprehensive results, including charting trends over time. Their initial study of charter school quality began in 2009; the latest was released in 2013.

Their findings confirm the pattern just discussed: Charters are more likely than conventional schools to be great. They are also more likely to be crummy. But the greats outnumber the crummies. And *overall,* charters are already as good as or better than conventional schools.

As the 2010-2011 school year closed, the average charter school student in the CREDO study had learned just as much math during the year as her average counterpart in a conventional school. And when it came to reading, the typical charter student had gained eight days of extra learning beyond what her non-charter counterpart absorbed.

Meanwhile, charters are getting better all the time. When the researchers compared the latest results to those from four years earlier, outcomes were improving significantly faster for charter students. The investigators concluded this steady improvement was being driven by the closure of poor charters and opening of more new high-performing charters every year.

And the Stanford investigators found, by the way, that the quality of a charter school can be predicted with a very high degree of accuracy by year three of the school's life. Schools that perform weakly from early on rarely improve, while those that start with a bang generally sustain their good results over the long run. All of this is an argument for philanthropists and authorizers to act energetically to upgrade the quality of charters—pulling the plug quickly on those that disappoint, and replacing them with offshoots of proven high-quality schools.

In addition to the fact that the charter sector is steadily upgrading, the other crisp and consequential finding of the CREDO studies is that charters are especially valuable to poor and minority children. In the words of a research summary: "This study found that public charter schools posted superior results with historically disadvantaged student populations. The study found that in nearly every category and subject area [charters] outperformed traditional public schools for the following student populations: Black, Hispanic, high-poverty, English-language learners, and special education."

Donors have signed on

If it is to become a large and permanent fix for our weak public education system, the charter sector will eventually need to include America's massive middle class within its field of action. For now, though, charter schools are lifting up precisely the kids who are most ill served by our education system. In the measured words of the Stanford professor who runs the CREDO lab, "results reveal that charter schools are benefiting low-income, disadvantaged students" in our major urban centers. In the view of most donors, that's the right place to start.

With undeniable accomplishments already piled up after just two decades of trial and error (in a social sector that has broken many a reformer's heart) charter schools have engendered true donor excitement. In the rest of this book, we'll look closely at how generous givers can make charter schools even more effective in the future. But first— to remind ourselves why further improvement is worth pursuing—let's look at how some of America's most savvy philanthropists assess the role of charter schools today:

> The No. 1 accomplishment of U.S. educational philanthropy over the last generation has been the growth of charter schools. —*Jim Blew, Walton Family Foundation*

> From my perspective, charter school growth is the only way out of today's education crisis. —*Victoria Rico, George Brackenridge Foundation*

> One place that charters have simply gotten better faster is in serving low-income kids. —*Katherine Bradley*

> Charter schools are the best thing that ever happened to education, because they provide competition to regular public schools and raise the bar that everyone is trying to attain. They provide thought leadership for other schools. So there's a multiplicative effect. —*Paul Tudor Jones*

Charters are the best opportunity we have. Because fixing school districts is something we've been trying to do, and failing at, for a hundred years. —*Reed Hastings*

Fiddling with curriculum, teacher evaluation, technology, or anything else will never produce dramatic student achievement gains in district schools. The single most important reform strategy you can undertake is to increase charter school quality and market share in your city, with the ultimate aim of turning your district into a charter school district.
—*Neerav Kingsland, New Schools for New Orleans*

Charter schools are a three-for-one: You get immediate good. You often get a model that can be replicated. And you put pressure on the larger system to evolve.
—*Caprice Young, Education Growth Group*

About 95 percent of the charter schools we've funded enable students to outperform comparable district schools in both math and reading; nearly 70 percent enable their students to outperform state averages even though they serve much higher than average percentages of low-income and minority students. So I believe that charters are eventually going to win. We'll look back and think that the time when people were assigned to certain schools was weird. —*Kevin Hall, Charter School Growth Fund*

Resist the temptation to think that charters are yesterday's reform. In fact, we're just getting started and really need donors committed to the idea of high-performing autonomous schools that give parents more choice. We need the next wave of donors to help build charters 2.0 or 3.0.
—*Christopher Nelson, Doris & Donald Fisher Fund*

Increasing the Supply of Good Charters

Good charter school operators have demonstrated they can consistently produce impressive results, in large volume, with the very same children who are floundering in conventional urban schools.

Charter schooling is no longer a theory. It's not in its experimental stage. It is a proven business model. But money and talent are now needed to build out additional schools in new markets.

As is always true when new enterprises are being expanded rapidly (whether it's coffee shops or schools), it will be important to pay close attention to quality while the number of establishments rises. That is the subject of the chapter after this one. Yet just as important as maintaining the quality of charters is opening more of them. If charters get good results but relatively few children have any chance of enrolling in one, today's vast pent-up demand for better schooling (a million kids already on waiting lists!) will never be met. Rather, charter schools will be educational boutiques—lovely, but too rare to be a solution to the widespread mediocrity of public education today—and a whole generation of children and parents will continue to despair over the poor options available to them.

Found, expand, or support

There are three basic paths open to donors who want to help increase the supply of charters: found new schools; expand existing schools; or aid schools indirectly through support organizations. All three are important, for reasons we'll touch on in the pages below.

Even philanthropists who lack large funds, or the time or knowledge to research the best models, can be helpful by pursuing the third option of indirect support. Nearly any donor can have important effects by giving money to charter school support groups with a strong track record. The Charter School Growth Fund, or the NewSchools Venture Fund— both of which invest the funds they pool from many sources into the highest-performing schools in the country—are easy options. A funder who wants to play a role in one of the cities where the charter school pot is boiling hardest could donate to New Schools for New Orleans, a group that has launched or expanded 28 schools in a little more than five years. Or you could join in league with others to aid one of the many regional organizations that incubate and undergird new charter schools all across America (ranging from the Mind Trust to Building Excellent Schools).

The middle option is to help existing high-quality school operators spread their successful formulas to additional campuses. Schools like those I will list later in this chapter in Tables 1 and 2 are some of the most effective new organizations of social uplift in the U.S.

They have rejected the many excuses peddled to explain why so many urban public schools are dismal today, and have used innovations like extended school days, unconventional teacher recruitment and training, pioneering work at blending computerized instruction into classrooms, extra involvement of families in the classroom, special character-building instruction for children, and simple higher expectations to get clearly better results. Rather than reinvent the wheel, some donors choose to back these proven racehorses.

Recently, most of the growth in charter school attendance has come in nonprofit schools that already have at least two campuses. Enrollment at multi-campus nonprofit schools roared upward by 50 percent in the latest year for which we have data. That's ten times as fast as the other two types of school—single campus, or for-profit—managed to grow.

Extrapolating from recent growth, I estimate that in 2014, as this book goes to press, the proportion of students in each of the three major types of charter schools is approximately as follows:

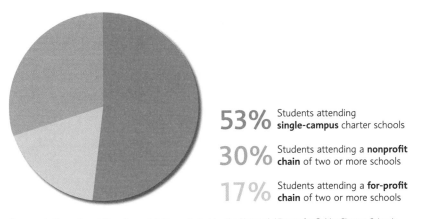

53% Students attending **single-campus** charter schools

30% Students attending a **nonprofit chain** of two or more schools

17% Students attending a **for-profit chain** of two or more schools

Source: Author extrapolations from statistics collected by the National Alliance for Public Charter Schools

While networks of nonprofit schools are today's booming sector, single-campus charter schools still provide the majority of seats at present. And the first option for expansion-minded philanthopists mentioned above—directly underwriting new solo schools—continues to offer exciting possibilities for "social invention." Many of the experts we consulted for this book say that while it's essential that existing networks of good schools be expanded as rapidly as possible, the charter school movement also needs additional startup operators and fresh approaches. (See the section "Continued school invention is necessary," below.)

The invention of new schools is not for dabblers, however. It requires patience, wisdom, diligence, and an eye for finding social entrepreneurs with creative ideas and the capacity to follow through on them. Donors must assess their successes and failures in this area honestly, for new creation from scratch is riskier than replicating existing schools or supporting intermediary organizations.

Active educational donors like the Walton Family Foundation do all of the above. They are loyal supporters of the many intermediary groups that help schools launch and grow. They provide startup funding for new individual charter schools "in the hopes of fostering the next great education breakthrough," as Walton educational adviser Bruno Manno puts it. And they help turn the crank that allows existing successes to reproduce themselves. "As long as huge backlogs of students remain on charter school waiting lists nationwide," says Manno, "expanding existing operators must remain an important part of our strategy."

New individual schools

New individual charter schools embody the inventive spirit of the charter school movement. When it comes to explaining why children learn in some settings but not others, there is still an enormous amount that we don't know or fully understand. Moreover, there is no single model for success in schooling. Children vary tremendously in family backgrounds, in innate capacities, in temperaments, and in cultural surroundings. There is both room and need for a wide range of schools in order to open learning avenues for every child.

New schools developed by passionate reformers working directly with children right in classrooms, without heavy bureaucratic regulation or encumberments of conventional practice, are prime laboratories for discovery. Given how often successful new charter schools continue to be created in what was previously thought to be unpromising soil, it is clear that we still have a lot to learn and invent, and that helping individual school entrepreneurs explore new formulas is a prime way to deepen our educational expertise.

If rebuilding American education one school at a time seems inefficient, remember that every successful new school has the potential to copy itself later in new locations. Trial and error experimentation in single schools, careful tracking of what has worked, and then rapid expansion is exactly how nearly all of today's most successful school networks—like KIPP, Uncommon Schools, BASIS, YES Prep, and others—originated. Very often, donors with business backgrounds serving on the boards of these schools were vital in creating the growth plans that guided the transition from upstart academy to network of successful schools. Inventing and launching new schools will always remain an important part of chartering, and philanthropists will necessarily play a central role in that process of creation, both with their money and with expertise and counsel.

One of the donors most active in creating new charter schools is the Walton Family Foundation. Walton's bread-and-butter educational-giving strategy since 1998 has been to make direct startup grants to new charters. These grants are directed to local community partners—a gifted educator, a group of parents, a collection of local business people, an effective nonprofit. Walton screens carefully for qualified entities within local communities, requiring them to provide a detailed business plan, evidence of broad community backing, a positive credit report, and strong potential for delivering excellent academic results. The foundation looks for strong governance, solid teacher recruitment, intelligent curricula, and good plans for testing and assessment. Once they've selected their partners, they are active in helping them design and build a high-quality school.

From 1997 until the end of 2012, Walton invested more than $311 million to support the creation of 1,437 schools. Their recipients primarily serve low-income families who do not have the resources to select private or high-performing district schools for their children. And to maximize its impact, the foundation targets certain states and cities where charter schools have the potential to achieve significant market share.

During their first decade, Walton "invested in charter schools wherever there was a decent law," according to Carrie Walton Penner. They had projects in 38 large cities. Then they homed in on locations where they felt they had their best chances of being transformative. "What we've done in the last

Though single-campus schools are still where a majority of charter students attend, most of the growth in charter schooling today is coming from expansion of successful multi-campus schools.

few years is really focus geographically," says Walton Penner. "We have seven districts where we're very deep. We work with innovative school leaders, in places where charter schools have a solid market share."

Christopher Nelson, who directs the Doris & Donald Fisher Fund, is also a fan of geographic concentration. His foundation's recent focal point has been New Orleans. "When funders flood a market and create lots of high-quality charter seats, we create a model that cannot be ignored."

Kevin Hall, president of the Charter School Growth Fund, likewise believes in the power of a critical mass. "Funders should make it a priority to create more cities where there's 20-30-40 percent share of students in charters. As we start seeing more metro areas where this is the case that will be a big 'aha!' moment."

Returning to the tactics of the Walton Family Foundation, two thirds of their school startup grants have been to stand-alone academies; the remainder built additional campuses for an existing school network. A typical grant will be $250,000. Subsequent awards are contingent on the school achieving performance goals. Schools that improve student achievement in reading, language arts, and math, as measured by reliable standardized tests, are what the foundation looks for. Regular assessments are required, with clear annual targets for improved student performance, and the foundation helps schools set strategies for refining their instruction methods to make sure they achieve those outcomes.

As an example of how timely philanthropy can kickstart a charter school, consider the Academy of Math and Science in Tucson, Arizona. Back in 2000, the Walton Family Foundation was researching ways to encourage new schools in Arizona (a hotbed for invention thanks to friendly charter school laws). Foundation officers discovered a nascent program serving 27 children in grades six through eight (most of them low income), housed in an old strip mall. The school was operating on a shoestring, but its founder was an impressive leader, an immigrant with advanced degrees and strong educational experience. She had created an education program based on E. D. Hirsch's Core Knowledge standards of classical learning, plus traditional standards used in European schools, where she had taught for ten years. This founder was determined to demonstrate that all students can succeed academically if well instructed under a clear and rigorous curriculum.

Walton made an initial grant of $150,000 to the school in 2000. After a subsequent review of academic and fiscal performance, a subsequent grant of $67,100 was offered in 2003. Those small sums were sufficient to get the institution launched as a public charter school. Today, the Academy of Math and Science (AMS) serves 334 K–8 students in Tucson, and its students pass Arizona's standardized statewide test at the highest rate of any school in its zip code.

AMS has earned an "A" rating from the Arizona Department of Education, the top distinction given by the state. The school is accredited by the American Academy for Liberal Education, and the original founder remains its director to this day. Two sister schools have been established, one in Tucson and one in Phoenix, enrolling an additional 354 children.

Many other charter networks grew out of single schools in this same way. Democracy Prep Charter School opened in New York City's central Harlem, quickly became the top-ranked public middle school in New York City, and was then expanded into a chain of nine high-performing schools sprinkled across New York and New Jersey. Newark's North Star Academy, opened in 1997, later grew into the Uncommon Schools charter network that now includes 38 schools in three states. The Amistad middle school in New Haven, Connecticut, eventually birthed today's 25-campus Achievement First network.

In creating new schools, Walton likes to join forces with other donors, and foundation staffers point out that even small givers can be helpful in the initial stages of launching a new school. An early grant of just $10,000 can go a long way toward helping a charter school develop part of its curriculum. That same sum might pay for crucial legal services needed during the startup phase. Or that amount provided by a small partner in support of a larger investor could simply be used to help create 10 additional seats at a school. Alternatively, a $10,000 gift to a statewide charter school association might make technical assistance and advocacy programs available to an entire region's charter schools. The point is that even modest gifts can go a long way in this kind of work, where funds are carefully husbanded.

Continued school invention is necessary

To those who might despair of saving the world one school at a time, Walton and other funders backing individual charter schools point out that all of the sector's most successful networks began their life as a single school. The long-term success of the charter sector, they argue, will depend on continued innovation in individual new schools, not just on expanding the scholastic chains that have already succeeded.

"We don't yet have enough high-quality models," agrees Neerav Kingsland of New Schools for New Orleans. "It would be unproductive for funders to get into the zero-sum game of simply recruiting the existing operator chains into their cities. Everyone can't just recruit everyone else's operators. The funding community needs to set up new high-quality operations." Kingsland acknowledges that "early-stage invention is higher risk, but funders have a responsibility to invest in it themselves rather than solely benefitting from someone else's early-stage investment."

Nina Rees, president of the National Alliance for Public Charter Schools, makes similar points. "We need to make sure we're open to the creation of future KIPPs and Success Academies. Replication won't provide enough supply, especially across multiple states with different populations and different policy environments."

"I don't think the charter movement wants to become totally a chain thing," suggests Chester Finn of the Thomas B. Fordham Foundation. "Mom-and-pop schools tailored to the needs of a particular community

> Most charter schools have heartbreakingly long waiting lists, and currently have to resort to lotteries to enroll students from this overlarge demand.

and affiliated with locally rooted institutions have merit. Moreover, the charter school movement doesn't benefit from having only big operators turn up at the state house when political decisions are afoot."

Kingsland, Rees, and Finn also strongly support multiplying successful schools, whether the task is turning one good school into three, or expanding a network of a dozen successful campuses into 50. "We need both replication and new," says Rees. Smart donors will have a practical strategy for turning the corner from invention into first-stage expansion. "Think about using funds to incentivize the single-site schools you support to grow, either slowly by adding grade levels, or more abruptly by adding new schools," suggests Christopher Nelson.

Reed Hastings, the Netflix founder who is also a major education donor and charter school strategist, suggests that "we need everybody who runs a great, single-site charter school to open one more. Just from one to two. The vast majority of charter schools are single-site schools. Those that have their sea legs, have operational sophistication, are doing well—these should be helped to open one more. And if the fives go to tens, and the tens to 20, that's a huge acceleration of the rate of growth of charter schools."

First, though, somebody needs to build a model worth copying. So in addition to making substantial startup grants of the sort that Walton and many other donors have offered to school inventors throughout the past two decades, some philanthropists provide planning grants and other forms of seed capital at an earlier stage of development. They find budding educational entrepreneurs who aren't yet at the point of erecting an academy, but have concepts and techniques they want to explore. This type of early assistance has encouraged the blossoming of many innovative new individual institutions.

For example, the William and Flora Hewlett Foundation and the Gates Foundation have pooled money in a venture called Next Generation Learning Challenges. Among other things, this organization gives prospective charter operators planning grants of $100,000 to help them design and develop schools. The special focus of this partnership of donors is blended learning, a new type of pedagogy combining online instruction and individualized teaching which is still in its very early days nationally. Their planning grants encourage creative approaches in the personalization of computerized learning. By germinating successful new charters schools in this field the donors hope to create powerful prototypes that educators in other places will be able to copy.

The Silicon Schools Fund is another group with a similar focus and a willingness to provide early seed capital for charter schools. They are on a path to fund 25 new schools throughout the San Francisco Bay area during the next five years. Their schools are required to have good plans for deploying computerized learning technologies in personalized ways. The fund hopes that these startups will eventually become exemplars of the power of online instruction to enhance student achievement and individual success.

Yet another funder encouraging charter school developers to deploy blended learning creatively is the Charter School Growth Fund. Its Next Generation School portfolio mostly subsidizes existing operators of successful charter schools (versus the new operators that Silicon Schools cultivates), helping them replicate good schools and bring proven charter school practices to more and more students.

Replication of existing schools

While creating new individual schools in cities across the country is essential to continued growth and innovation in the charter sector, this slow creative process cannot meet existing public demand by itself. Most charter schools have heartbreakingly long waiting lists, and currently have to resort to lotteries to enroll students from this overlarge demand. To come closer to matching public appetites (while also becoming a bigger influence on the direction of public education more broadly) the charter school sector also needs to spin off reproductions of its existing successful schools as rapidly as funds and dedicated educators can be procured.

In some cities, funders conclude that the surest and fastest way to add high-quality school seats is to take existing schools with well-tested features and launch them in bulk. Donors are in essence extending the reach of existing charter school "brands" by creating franchises.

Most strong industries feature compelling brands. Consumers come to know a brand and what characteristics it offers. The brand is a shortcut to consistent, predictable delivery of those desired qualities. Brands not only signal valuable information to consumers, they also create powerful incentives for their owners to maintain quality so that the brand name remains strong. In addition, brands can achieve economies of scale that make them more efficient than stand-alone labels.

Organizations that oversee a string of charter schools can provide services they've pioneered and tested in other locales, lending a substantial degree of confidence in their workability. The umbrella managers can offer local educators curriculum and procedures, means of teacher recruitment, and physical facilities. Headquarters can often provide these things at less cost and effort through their standing infrastructure. There's no need to reinvent the wheel on book and technology buying, payroll services, food and transportation management, health benefits, and such—guidance can be gotten from the operator's home office.

In certain aspects, all good multi-campus charter operators resemble each other. The operator's most important role may be to enforce quality control. If a particular school is not performing, it not only disappoints the children in its classrooms, it threatens the reputation of the operator. The overarching operator thus is less likely to accept excuses from on-scene managers than might be the case if there was no larger brand to protect.

All of these reasons have fueled the expansion of today's best-known charter school networks. The demonstrated successes of those networks at repeating their formula in new places have created excitement and energy. The result has been to extend many chains of high-quality charters across state and regional boundaries during the past several years.

In education jargon, these school chains are referred to as either charter management organizations (CMOs) or education management organizations (EMOs). The central difference: CMOs are nonprofit; EMOs are for-profit.

In the past few years, nonprofit operators have been opening schools at a faster clip than for-profit firms, but there are lots of schools under both umbrellas. As the year 2014 opens, we estimate that close to 1,400 charter schools are operating under the management of some nonprofit network, and that about 800 charter schools (plus several large online aggregations of students) are managed by one of today's for-profit networks. The remaining 4,200 charter schools are freestanding institutions or in very small school groups.

When discussing charter school networks, this book focuses more on nonprofit operators, simply because they are the ones philanthropists most often collaborate with (along with the individual, non-network schools). Table 1, below, lists some of today's large and otherwise prominent nonprofit operators of charter schools. Because these networks are growing so rapidly, the numbers of schools and students listed will soon be outdated, but these figures are current as of roughly the beginning of 2014.

Some large nonprofit charter school operators	
KIPP Schools	141 schools and 51,000 students in 21 states, and counting
Aspire Schools	37 schools and 14,000 students in California and Tennessee
Uncommon Schools	38 high-scoring schools in New York, New Jersey, and Massachusetts, serving about 9,000 students
Options for Youth	34 alternative schools in California
Concept Schools	30 science-focused schools in seven states
Summit Academies	27 schools in Ohio
Achievement First	25 schools enrolling 8,100 in three states
Constellation Schools	22 large schools in Ohio
YES Prep	13 campuses and 8,000 students in Houston, with 10 more schools on the way in Tennessee and Louisiana
Success Academies	22 high-performing NYC schools enrolling 6,000 students, on a path to 40 campuses

Alliance College-ready Public Schools	22 Los Angeles schools with 10,000+ students
Lighthouse Academies	21 schools in eight states
Green Dot Schools	20 schools, most in L.A., more than 10,000 students
Great Hearts Academies	16 schools in metropolitan Phoenix, to become 22, including new states
Mastery Schools	15 Philadelphia academies, mostly "turnarounds" of failed conventional public schools
BASIS Schools	12, soon to be 15, top-ranked schools in Arizona, Texas, and Washington D.C.
Chicago International	15 schools in Chicago, one in Rockford, Illinois
UNO Network	16 Chicago schools oriented to 7,500 Hispanic children
IDEA Schools	30 schools in Texas, on a path to 56 by 2017
Noble Network	15 Chicago campuses with 9,000 students
Uplift Education	13 high-rated Dallas-Fort Worth schools
PUC Schools	13 campuses in southern California
High Tech High	(12 schools and 5,200 pupils in San Diego, with a special focus on math, engineering, and practical technical careers
Richard Milburn Academy	11 alternative high schools in Texas and Florida
Friendship Schools	10 schools in D.C. and Maryland
Rocketship Education	10 high-scoring schools in California, Wisconsin, and Tennessee, with others on the way for Indiana, Louisiana, Texas, and D.C.
Breakthrough Schools	nine campuses in Cleveland
STRIVE Prep	nine Denver-area schools
LEARN School Network	eight schools in Chicago
Summit Schools	seven Bay Area schools, with more on the way
DSST Public Schools	six well-regarded science and technology schools in Denver area

The for-profit twist

While nonprofit chains are currently growing much faster than for-profit counterparts, many school reformers believe for-profit operators can be helpful in the race to improve public education. By more than 2:1, the education experts polled for this book by The Philanthropy Roundtable said they believe that "for-profit entities that manage charter schools hold promise to grow the sector in a positive way." The 69 percent of respondents expressing that positive view of for-profits were then asked whether they thought philanthropy has a part to play in supporting for-profit charters; 88 percent said yes.

The main downside to being a for-profit is the potential to be demagogued for "making money on the backs of school children," as opponents of charter schools like to charge. But there is a clear demand for-profit school operators. The growth charted in Table 2 makes that clear.

Examples of national for-profit charter school operators	
National Heritage Academies	76 schools in nine states
Imagine Schools	in 13 states serving more than 30,000 students
Charter Schools USA	58 schools in seven states
Leona Group	20,000+ students in five states
Mosaica Education	12 states, and also overseas
Altair Learning	10,000 students
Insight Schools	operating in seven states
Academica	not an operator, but a provider of essential services and management support, working in 100 schools in five states plus D.C.

Note that some cutting-edge nonprofits like BASIS are experimenting with operating at least partly under for-profit rules. All of the current BASIS charter schools are nonprofits, but the overarching management and development firm was set up some years ago as a for-profit. (Carpe Diem Schools is moving toward a similar division.) The for-profit company secures the charters, employs the teachers, and handles centralized functions. Among other benefits, this allows the schools to create 401(k) plans for teachers instead of pushing them into public retirement systems, and opens access to private capital markets, which could speed expansion.

To supplement its superb public charter schools, BASIS has also set up a new "BASIS Independent" division on a for-profit basis to run moderately priced private schools. Private schools make better economic sense in some locations. At current BASIS charter schools, state payments per child come in at close to half of what conventional public schools in those same regions receive. Charging tuition is one way to get around those unfairly low reimbursement rates.

A private school also isn't handcuffed by rules that sometimes squeeze charter schools. These include things like imposing union bargaining agreements, or prohibiting teachers who lack official certifications. One of the secrets to the success of BASIS has been hiring teachers who are content experts (like retired engineers, or former writing instructors), even if they don't have traditional credentials.

The first two BASIS Independent schools are located in Brooklyn in New York City and San Jose, California. The San Jose school will serve 800 students, with tuition costing $22,000. The Brooklyn facility in the Red Hook neighborhood will have 1,000 seats for K–12, and annual tuition of $23,500. After opening in fall 2014 both schools will grow in stages toward their full enrollments.

The reality is that there are excellent and poor schools operating under both for-profit and nonprofit models. The tax status of the umbrella organization running a charter school should not be a vital factor. The best charter

> The reality is that there are excellent and poor schools operating under both for-profit and nonprofit models.

operators—nonprofits and for-profits alike—are very business-like. Many are famous for squeezing pennies out of their operations, especially on the bricks-and-mortar side, so they can invest more in instruction.

Victoria Rico, chairwoman of the George Brackenridge Foundation which turned San Antonio into a hotbed of charter school growth, describes how for-profit financial controls can translate into academic performance:

> In addition to several nonprofits, we have two for-profit operations among the schools we brought to San Antonio. One is BASIS Schools. Their financial savvy is a big part of their success. They are really good at building inexpensively, at staffing lean, and keeping costs down generally. Their schools don't need a lot of land. They make do with half a gym, for instance, and they don't worry about crowded classrooms. It's all about high-quality teachers for them—which they are able to attract because they

are an uber-cool place for an entrepreneurial instructor to work. They don't waste a lot of leadership time reinventing processes. They focus on academics, not fancy facilities, and their successes feed on themselves. So even though they produce top results, and came here as a for-profit, they are about the least expensive school to replicate. It's amazing.

Nina Rees of the National Alliance for Public Charter Schools urges that "philanthropists should support for-profit operators to the extent they can. These organizations understand growth better than everyone else. Encouraging them will help the movement expand much faster."

"At times it can be politically challenging to promote for-profits, because of a few bad apples and exaggerated criticisms from opponents that have given 'profit' an unfair bad rap in anything educational. But it shouldn't matter what your tax status is as long as you are running an effective charter school," states Rees. "Laws are unfriendly to for-profits in many states now. This needs to change, because they know scale and how to reach it, and we need them."

If for-profit investors are able to deliver consistent student achievement along with a steady flow of earnings, this will be a much more sustainable way to create new charter schools in the future, and it will draw both private capital and top managers into public education—which at present is badly undersupplied with both of those valuable resources. Donors willing to provide start-up funding to for-profit school operators when they are embryonic businesses might produce large benefits down the road.

When bringing in a multi-campus operator may be smart

One niche where it may prove useful to bring in a proven charter school is for "restarting" a failing charter school. Every charter school is supposed to uphold a compact with local taxpayers—the school gains considerable autonomy from the usual bureaucratic restraints, and in return is accountable for producing better-than-ordinary results. As in every other human endeavor though, some charter schools disappoint. If charters are going to be defensible as a more effective alternative to conventional schools, then it is important to shut down those that don't deliver.

The problem is, shutting down a school can be very disruptive to the students and local families involved. A "restart" that brings in fresh managers without locking the doors to children and families already engaged with the school can be less troublesome. It is the equivalent of your local grocery store or familiar airline continuing to serve customers even while new management sweeps in to establish all-new operations.

Putting unproven educators at the helm during this tricky process may not have much appeal for a school's overseers, though. Installing one of the successful networks to replicate their formula instead may be more attractive. The school can continue to serve the same students, without closure, even while strong yet low-risk action is being taken to protect the expectation that a charter school should be more than mediocre.

The chain operator, meanwhile, doesn't have to find and equip a building, or recruit a student body from scratch. He can focus on establishing the culture, curriculum, and teaching standards that allowed him to succeed in other places. So a "school restart replication" can sometimes be attractive to authorizers, parents and children, and school operators alike. (I touch again on school restarts later in this book, in the discussions of Mastery Schools in Philadelphia and the Achievement School District in Tennessee.)

There is another niche where donors might decide to clone existing charter schools rather than inventing new ones: in places where a state is at or near a binding cap on the number of charters allowed to open. Currently, 22 states impose an arbitrary limit on the number of charter schools they allow to operate. Texas is one.

The problems this can cause are illustrated in San Antonio. As in lots of other large cities, the educational outlook in San Antonio is grim for many minority and poor children. Only 60 percent of students in the city's conventional public schools graduate from high school, and only ten percent of those will graduate from college within six years after starting.

With those stark figures in mind, San Antonio's Brackenridge Foundation decided to take some dramatic action. The foundation set a bold goal: use the local nonprofit Choose to Succeed to bring 80,000 new high-quality charter school seats to the city. Choose to Succeed helps charters in many ways. They aid the financing of new facilities (local banks treat the endorsement of Choose to Succeed as a quality stamp). They help in recruiting teachers and students. They offer introductions to neighborhood leaders, school officials, and businesspeople. They lend political support. An ally like this can greatly ease the process of locating and nurturing the sorts of star educators capable of establishing a high-functioning school from scratch.

The Brackenridge board and chairwoman Victoria Rico, however, had to adapt their giving strategy to a harsh reality. The Texas legislature had passed a cap saying there would be no more than 215 charters allowed in the state, and very few slots remained. The sole source of wiggle room: once an operator receives a charter, that operator is permitted to replicate its schools in other places. Brackenridge realized that rather than start brand-new schools that would bang into the statewide cap, they needed to convince high-quality chains to expand to San Antonio, where one charter would allow them to open numerous campuses.

"We'd like to be able to support individual, startup charter schools," says Rico. "But it simply isn't practical in Texas, with the charter cap. We have to do whatever it takes to improve educational outcomes for our students. And for the time being, pursuing only charter operators equipped to replicate multiple schools under a single charter is our most promising option."

Fortunately, that still leaves many great options. "I started out learning about KIPP, and slowly began to understand that KIPP was just one flavor that the sector had to offer. I am astonished by the diversity of models that exist and the results that so many have been able to achieve," states Rico. So far Brackenridge has made great progress in drawing top operators like KIPP, IDEA, BASIS, Great Hearts, Rocketship, and Carpe Diem to San Antonio.

Some progress has recently been made on the policy front. During the summer of 2013, the Texas legislature voted to gradually raise the state's cap on charter schools—to 305 by the year 2019. That offers an opportunity for the Brackenridge Foundation and other givers to encourage a more natural mix of new educational entrepreneurs and replicators. In the meantime, multi-campus networks have been saviors in Texas.

A brief look at some fast-expanding nonprofit charter school networks

The national brand that has probably received support from more funders than any other is KIPP Schools. This mushrooming network (141 schools in 20 states plus DC as of late 2013) currently serves 51,000 students, and is in the process of growing much larger. All KIPP leaders undergo a common training program, and every school subscribes to a set of principles called the "five pillars." These emphasize high expectations; a longer school day; a commitment among students, parents, and staff to put in more than ordinary effort; a devolution of authority and resources to local principals and teachers so they can act quickly and flexibly; and a no-excuses focus on student performance, as demonstrated on standardized tests.

KIPP's headquarters provides individual schools with regular support and guidance, and monitors whether schools are implementing the five pillars faithfully and getting strong results. But each school operates independently or as part of a city-level network. The considerable autonomy they grant to local managers leads some researchers to describe KIPP as employing the "franchise" model.

The most impressive fact about KIPP is their consistent, superior student performance. Though 86 percent of KIPP students are low-income, and 95 percent are African American or Latino, more than 93 percent of those who complete eighth grade in a KIPP school graduate from high school, and over 83 percent go on to college. In conventional public schools with similar demographics, the college matriculation rate is 20 percent. KIPP students complete bachelor's degrees at rates higher than the general U.S. population, and at four times the rate of other students from poor communities.

Never satisfied, KIPP is constantly appraising and refining its operations. For instance, when the organization noticed that two thirds of their first alumni cohorts who enrolled in college failed to complete their higher education on schedule, analysis was undertaken to see what they could do to make certain their students not only enter college but then stay there through graduation. KIPP has also discovered that they can have a stronger positive effect on neighborhoods and cities when they cluster schools more tightly and build up a high-aspiration educational culture throughout a region, rather than plunking orphaned schools all across the country. (This illustrates one of the strengths of a replication strategy—the experienced operators have had time to adapt and evolve their techniques in ways that can improve outcomes.)

Another very successful charter management organization that is expanding to meet rippling public demand is Achievement First, which operates a string of schools in New York, Connecticut, and Rhode Island. Starting in 2003 with one school in Connecticut, Achievement First had by 2013 expanded (with philanthropic help) to 25 elementary, middle, and high schools, with more to come. The Achievement First network currently serves some 8,100 heavily poor and minority students.

Achievement First has made remarkable progress with its children. On the 2012 New York state math assessment, 88 percent of its pupils achieved proficiency, compared to 60 percent of all students in New

York City, and a 65 percent of all students statewide. In language arts, 58 percent of Achievement First students achieved proficiency, versus 47 percent of all New York City students and 55 percent of all students in New York. In Connecticut, 61 percent of Achievement First high schoolers who took the Advanced Placement U.S. History exam scored a 4 or 5 (5 is the top score), compared with only 33 percent of students across the U.S. Remarkably, more than 75 percent of Achievement First high-school graduates receive a college bachelor's degree within six years of graduating high school. (The overall college graduation rates for African-American and Latino adults are 18 percent and 11 percent respectively.)

A third highly impressive charter network now in the process of replicating itself on additional campuses is Uncommon Schools. At present, the organization serves about 9,000 students at 38 charter schools across

> KIPP students complete bachelor's degrees at rates higher than the general U.S. population, and at four times the rate of other students from poor communities.

Massachusetts, New Jersey, and New York. Eight out of ten of its students are low-income, and 98 percent are African-American or Hispanic.

Like other fast-growing high-quality charter operators, Uncommon Schools gets remarkable results with its underprivileged children. In recent years, Uncommon closed 56 percent of the achievement gap between its African-American students and white students in the same state. In 2012, 100 percent of the network's high-school seniors took the SAT exam, and they achieved an average score 72 points above the national average.

Aspire Public Schools was one of the very first charter management organizations. Netflix founder and entrepreneur par excellence Reed Hastings put up the original money and many of the ideas that animated Aspire. Its formula took immediate root, and within 15 years of its 1998 startup it was educating 14,000 students annually in 37 schools. As a group, Aspire's students significantly outperform the average score on California's statewide achievement exams, and they come out head and shoulders above comparable low-income students in conventional schools. Two thirds of Aspire schools, with their heavily minority and low-income student bodies, have already exceeded the state target for "academic excellence." Indeed, if you treat Aspire as its own school district, it ranks in the top 5 percent for performance and achievement, when compared to similar size districts all across California.

What is most impressive about Aspire schools is that they get better and better every single year. On California's Academic Performance Index, Aspire's total score has increased, without fail, each year since the network was founded. In 1999, Aspire students averaged 406 on this statewide assessment. By 2005, that was up to 520. In 2010, Aspire students reached 648, and their results jumped further to 720 in 2011, and 780 in 2012—a remarkable record of relentless improvement. And here's a more practical statistic: Throughout the past four years, 100 percent of Aspire's thousands of graduates have secured admission to a four-year college.

Rocketship Education, also originating from Silicon Valley, is a fifth example of a fast-expanding charter school manager. The brainchild of philanthropist and Silicon Valley CEO John Danner, it is well known as a pioneer in the field of blended learning—mixing computerized instruction and face-to-face tutoring to create highly personalized instruction for each student. Like many other charters, Rocketship focuses primarily on low-income and urban students, many of them not native English speakers. Unlike some, its blended learning model requires fewer teachers, which gives it economic advantages that have made it easier to expand. And Rocketship achieves better results than comparable conventional schools.

Rocketship's first school opened in San Jose in 2007. Its success soon led to a total of eight Rocketship schools in the city, serving 4,500 pupils. Despite this rapid growth, the organization still has 2,500 families on its waiting list, hoping to enroll children. (For details on how Rocketship's classrooms and schools operate, see *Blended Learning: A Wise Giver's Guide to Supporting Tech-assisted Teaching* published by The Philanthropy Roundtable.)

In 2013, Rocketship opened its first school in Milwaukee. With strong support from the Lynde and Harry Bradley Foundation, a $1 million expansion grant from the Eli and Edythe Broad Foundation, technical help from the Gates Foundation, and investments from many other donors, Rocketship will open eight high-quality schools in Milwaukee over the next five years, and another eight in Nashville, where its first school opens in 2014. The organization has also won charters to operate in New Orleans, Indianapolis, Memphis, and Washington, D.C. Their goal is to eventually operate in 50 cities and serve one million children. The combination of broad philanthropic backing and Rocketship's low-cost business model is what makes this expansion conceivable.

Rocketship's financially attractive model gets results. Even though 90 percent of its students are low income, and 75 percent come from non-English speaking homes, fully 80 percent of Rocketeers score at the "proficient" or "advanced" level for math on the California Standards Test. That's nearly the same as the 83 percent rate achieved in California's ten most affluent districts.

The BASIS charter school network is yet another high-performing group now undergoing expansion with help from givers. It operates a dozen schools, with more in the works, in Arizona, Texas, and D.C. (For a glimpse into BASIS classrooms, see pages 70-74 of *Closing America's High-achievement Gap: A Wise Giver's Guide to Helping Our Most Talented Students Reach Their Full Potential,* from The Philanthropy Roundtable.)

"There's no magic here. It's just a four-letter word: Work. We just work harder," says network co-founder Michael Block. BASIS administers a rigorous, A.P.-based curriculum to all students, across the board. Craig Barrett, former CEO of the Intel Corporation, has been a key philanthropic supporter of BASIS. He explains in an interview that, "We start on the premise that any fourth-grade child who is at grade level can come to BASIS and succeed in our accelerated program."

The network's intent is to challenge every single student. "We have been severely underestimating all kids," argues Block. Science is a particular focus of BASIS schools. In sixth grade, students begin taking biology, chemistry, and physics as separate subjects. Math is also a sharp focus. All students will have completed Algebra I by the end of their seventh-grade year. Beginning in sixth grade, students are required to pass comprehensive exams in all core subjects in order to be promoted to the next grade.

This mirrors the demanding course schedule of many top-performing European and Asian schools. To build the right culture and expectations from the start at the new BASIS satellite in D.C., the network imported several experienced instructors from its Arizona flagship schools. BASIS negotiates an initial salary individually with each teacher. It also offers performance-based financial incentives. Teachers of A.P. courses, for instance, earn an additional $100 for every student who makes a grade of four on the A.P. exam, and an additional $200 for every student who earns a five (the top score). Rather than traditional sick days, BASIS gives teachers a "Wellness Bonus" of $1,500. They lose a predetermined amount of that for each sick-day taken.

The results of all of this are outstanding. On the 2012 Arizona assessment test, BASIS students outperformed statewide averages in math, reading, writing, and science in every tested grade. The *average* BASIS student takes 10 AP exams, and the typical score is 3.9. In 2012, BASIS students outscored national averages on A.P. exams in 23 different subjects.

Approximately 1.5 million American students take the PSAT test every year, and on the basis of its scores about one percent of all high-school seniors are selected as National Merit Scholar Finalists. In 2012, *more than 25 percent* of all BASIS seniors earned that high recognition. International tests like the PISA exam show that BASIS students are competitive with the very best scholars anywhere in the world.

Though they have to date focused on middle schools and high schools, BASIS is now piloting a kindergarten-to-fourth-grade school in Tucson, Arizona. So a full K–12 system will soon exist under their model. The network's major goal is to maintain its extremely high and consistent level of quality as it continues to grow with philanthropic support. And growth is a high priority for the network's leadership. "All cities should have a BASIS," according to the chain's managers.

A quite different charter school operator now in expansion mode is Great Hearts Academies. It created a string of Arizona campuses that produce impressive results. Great Hearts offers an academically rigorous, classical liberal arts education with an emphasis on the great books. As of 2013, it had 16 schools operating in the Phoenix area, and more on the way, including one in Texas. There are currently more than 9,000 students on waiting lists hoping to attend one of the Great Hearts facilities. (Consult *Closing America's High-achievement Gap* for more details on this school's operations.)

Great Hearts has no electives. All students take the same challenging sequence in math, science, foreign language, fine arts, and human-

> There's no magic here. It's just a four-letter word: Work. We just work harder. We start on the premise that any fourth-grade child who is at grade level can come to BASIS and succeed.

ities. Students learn Algebra I in seventh grade, which puts them all on path for calculus in eleventh and twelfth grade. Three years of Latin begin in sixth grade. Medieval history is required in eighth grade, and music and poetry in ninth and tenth. The "core reading list" for elementary students includes *Don Quixote, Gulliver's Travels, Treasure Island*, and *Narrative of the Life of Frederick Douglass*. For middle and high school, the list includes *The Aeneid, As I Lay Dying, Crime and Punishment, Federalist #10, Henry V, Plessy v. Ferguson*, and *The Republic*.

Great Hearts also forms its students morally, seeking to "graduate thoughtful leaders of character who will contribute to a more philosophical, humane, and just society." Students wear uniforms and adhere to an honor code. The schools try to instill nine core virtues in students: humility, integrity, friendship, perseverance, wisdom, courage, responsibility, honesty, and citizenship. One "philosophical pillar" of the network's culture is that "sarcasm, bad will, and apathy are toxic to the work of teaching and learning." Great Hearts vigorously recruits instructors it believes will be exceptional classrooms leaders, regardless of their backgrounds or state certifications. "We place stock in content expertise and pedagogy, which don't necessarily track with teacher credentialing," states donor and co-founder Jay Heiler.

On 2012 statewide assessments, Great Hearts students outperformed the average Arizona student in every tested subject and every grade level. Of its five high schools with 2012 graduating classes, between 83 and 97 percent of seniors were headed to four-year colleges. Fully 13 percent of all seniors at Chandler Prep, one of the network's high schools, were named National Merit Scholarship Finalists.

Replicating at an earlier stage

Funders who want to nurture strong schools that are at an earlier stage of expansion than the national brands described in the last section also have opportunities. They can provide growth capital to schools that have proven themselves locally but exist on only a few campuses. The charter school movement is still at an early stage, and many additional star operators are likely to emerge in the years ahead. Savvy donors can help identify and propel these nascent operations.

As mentioned earlier, even today's largest and most impressive charter chains all began as solo operations. Aspire Public Schools had only 200 students in one charter school as its first school year came to a close in 2000. Today it has 12,000 students in California alone.

In Chicago, Noble Street College Prep opened in 1999, and only became an operator of multiple campuses after its success brought calls for more such classrooms, and a willingness among donors to help pay for them. Today, the Noble Network of charter schools is still entirely Chicago-centered, but it has grown to 15 campuses—with plans to continue its rapid growth so it can educate 15 percent of Chicago's public high school students by 2020.

Or consider the trajectory of YES Prep. In 1995, a group of parents, teachers, and community leaders alarmed by the dysfunction at Rusk elementary school in Houston created Project YES. Under the leadership of Teach for America corps member Christopher Barbic, in 1998 this became YES College Preparatory School, a charter middle and high school. Two years later, this little sprout housed in trailers on a deserted parking lot had become the top-performing high school in Texas.

That caught the eye of local philanthropists. The Brown Foundation made a generous gift in 2001 that allowed the school to move to a permanent site. Fully 100 percent of the first class of seniors earned acceptances at a four-year college, though 86 percent had no previous college attendees in their family. Then in 2003 the George Foundation of Fort Bend County gave YES a grant to copy its formula in a second and third school. By 2005 YES Prep was not only attracting repeat support from local donors, but also its first national funding from backers like the Gates Foundation. Today, with 8,000 students in Houston on 13 campuses and phenomenal results that have it ranked as one of the top schools in the U.S., YES Prep is busily preparing to launch itself into Louisiana and Tennessee, and very likely other states after that.

There are at present lots of very fine charter schools with just one campus, or a handful of locations in neighborhoods of a single city. These could be ramped up by donors willing to help the proprietors repeat their successes in new buildings. Just a few quick examples of the kind of solo operations or tiny chains that could potentially be scaled up:

- E. L. Haynes in Washington, D.C.
- DC Prep, also in the district
- DaVinci Schools, four highly innovative charters in Los Angeles
- Match Education, with five small schools in Boston

- Brooke Charter School, a three-school operation in Boston with 3,700 families on its waiting list
- Brighter Choice, a group of schools in Albany, New York, that includes single-sex elementary and middle schools for both boys and girls
- the Tindley Network, just transitioning from one school to several in Indianapolis

It is also sometimes possible for a donor to draw a large charter school operator into a significant new field, where their operational excellence can bring good education to an entirely different population. An example would be the Early Years Initiative of Washington, D.C.'s CityBridge Foundation. An important part of this program was to help KIPP and DC Prep set up their first efforts at early-childhood education. Between 2008 and 2012, approximately $3.5 million of CityBridge funding was allocated to these top-rated operators to allow them to create excellent pre-K programs (their first efforts with that age group) in the nation's capital.

The initiative has had great success: children from disadvantaged backgrounds who enter the program as three-year-olds leave for kindergarten on roughly equal academic footing with peers from middle-class households. Katherine Bradley, co-founder and president of CityBridge, believes that charter schools offer the best vehicle for early-childhood schooling, just as they so often do at the primary and secondary level. "We decided to do our work through charter schools," she says, "because that's where we found partners with the capacity to innovate, run more than one school, and grow a great idea onto a larger scale."

Intermediary organizations that donors could support

Some donors may choose to invest in charter schools indirectly, by pooling their funds with charter school intermediaries in ways that allow them to help many different schools simultaneously. Intermediary organizations expand the industry not by establishing schools of their own but by providing funding, expertise, and assistance to numerous founders, sponsoring groups, or existing schools so they can successfully create, expand, or sustain operations. Intermediaries provide research, practical guidance, and advice to school creators, while also holding them accountable.

Venture philanthropy groups such as the NewSchools Venture Fund and the Charter School Growth Fund are intermediaries that funnel hundreds of millions of philanthropic dollars to charter schools. Both are demanding partners—only about 9 percent of the schools that apply for funding from CSGF are accepted. The rigorous ways that these two groups scrutinize potential partners can be instructive to donors.

Both organizations use multi-stage assessment processes to vet organizations for possible investment. CSGF does a "blind" quantitative analysis which compares the academic performance of the candidate to comparable organizations. Then they look carefully at the leadership team, the school's academic philosophy, its operating model, its financial viability, and its potential to grow.

NewSchools begins by ensuring that a school fits its current investment strategy, will serve low-income students, has the ability to sustain itself and grow, and may eventually be able to have a positive influence beyond the students directly served. Schools that pass these first screenings then get evaluated for their management team, financial model, quality of product, and local market demand. Both of these funds typically invest in a small number of organizations and make large multi-year commitments.

The candidates who are finally selected receive not only money but also intensive early-stage help with planning and strategy. Schools that then perform well become eligible for larger and larger grants to help spur expansions. The philanthropic capital that these intermediaries inject early on generally allows the recipient charter schools to become excellent right from the outset. That attracts students, and the public funding which follows them, and helps schools become self-supporting quickly. "Our value is not only in aggregating funds and providing practical services, but also in providing first-class management assistance to the operators of these schools," summarized Ted Mitchell while he was CEO of NewSchools.

Charter school incubators are another class of intermediaries that can be enormously helpful when setting up a new school. Launching a school from scratch requires successful accomplishment of many tasks. One must recruit and train teachers. A physical facility has to be procured, and made useable. Operating procedures on everything from educational principles to discipline to food service must be established. There are books and furnishings and technology to buy and install. It is necessary to organize a board of directors. State laws have to be understood and followed. There are always funds to be raised.

Realizing that it can be difficult to handle all of this without being overwhelmed, the charter sector has responded by creating organizations called incubators. These provide a paycheck to aspiring new charter leaders as they train in important skills that running a new school will require. Most incubators are very selective, and choose a small number of promising leaders who are willing to commit to a one- or two-year fellowship, and then meet certain guidelines while running their school. In addition to their classroom training, incubators offer lots of nitty-gritty help in areas like getting to know local regulators, politicians, and community stakeholders. After the fellowship ends, the leaders launch their schools—with the continuing support and assistance of the incubating organization.

> Recent studies show that when charter schools start off poorly, they rarely become good performers later on.

It is risky to launch a school with underprepared leaders. Recent studies show that when charter schools start off poorly, they rarely become good performers later on. (See the CREDO findings in Chapter 1.) Conversely, those schools that start off with a bang tend to remain high performers over time. "To improve quality, funders would be wise to invest in incubation organizations that help new schools get off on the right foot," suggests Neerav Kingsland.

So it is very good news that recent years have seen a rapid growth of incubator organizations. Thanks to expanded incubation, funded by philanthropy, some cities have been able to set much higher targets for the number of new high-quality charter seats they'll have available in the future. Following are examples of the sorts of incubators that have helped fuel this progress:

- Building Excellent Schools has a strong record as an incubator of more than 50 high-quality schools, in 12 states so far. They offer intensive one-year fellowships that support carefully selected participants to spend a year designing and then launching an urban charter school. All of the schools they incubate are customized to their community, and operated independently (not in any of the established management chains). Fellows do a residency in a successful

operating charter school, and visit more than 30 of the highest
performing charter schools in the Northeast during their
training, which is centered in Boston. An alumni network,
regular summits, annual awards, and follow-up training are
offered to extend the support and sharing of information far
beyond the initial incubation period.

- The Mind Trust awards $1 million grants to carefully selected
  educational entrepreneurs willing to found and lead excellent
  new charter schools in Indianapolis. Through their incubator
  program the group aims to bring 10,000 new high-quality charter
  seats to Indianapolis. Some of its awards have gone to operators
  like Rocketship and KIPP to help them bring their models to
  city. Other funding has gone to create new school concepts, like
  Phalen Academies, a startup built on a blended-learning model.
  Mind Trust supporters who have made this incubator possible
  include about a hundred individual donors and 36 foundation or
  corporate donors in recent years—ranging from the Lilly, Gates,
  Broad, and Walton foundations to Cummins Inc. and Kroger.

- Get Smart Schools is an incubator that aspires to prepare
  85 new school leaders and launch at least 50 autonomous
  schools across Colorado. Its tools include a yearlong
  leadership training program for men and women aiming
  to open schools, an even more detailed fellowship program
  which brings educational entrepreneurs right to the moment
  of starting or taking over a school, plus a state-approved
  alternative program for licensing principals. Of the 15
  new schools (enrolling 5,000 students) that Get Smart
  has incubated far enough to gather performance data, 12
  are already getting more achievement growth out of their
  students than the average school in their district, despite
  enrolling a student population that is 76 percent in poverty.
  The incubator encourages the schools in its network to keep
  their standards high by awarding the "Get Smart Schools"
  mark to those with excellent results.

- Charter School Partners intends to help launch 20 new schools
  in Minnesota during the next five years, while simultaneously
  helping its 30 existing partner schools move "from good to
  great" in as many academic areas as possible. Donors have
  included the Carlson Family Foundation, Best Buy's Children's

Foundation, General Mills, the Minneapolis Foundation, Cargill, other organizations, and many individual donors.

- Tennessee Charter School Incubator focuses on two urban areas within the state: Nashville and Memphis. It was the first incubator to operate across a state instead of just in one city. Prospective school leaders get intensive preparation in the management, academic, and entrepreneurial skills needed to run an academy. Like other charter incubators, it seeks partners whose credentials indicate their school is likely to be demanding and high performing. The organization's goal is to bring 20,000 new high-quality charter seats to Tennessee. In 2012 the new schools it helped open outscored metropolitan Nashville Public Schools by at least 10 percentage points in every subject tested on the state's annual assessment.

- New Schools for New Orleans is a major reason that nearly 80 percent of all students in New Orleans now attend a charter school. NSNO offers local educational entrepreneurs the intensive training and management services that all good incubators feature, as well as teacher instruction, help with recruiting and screening board members, and intensive financial, legal, and operations support. It supports both new individual schools and expanding chain schools. In addition, NSNO has taken on an influential leadership role in Louisiana educational politics. It works to improve charter-related policies, and helps state authorities design processes that encourage excellence and equity in New Orleans schools.

An effort that offers charters equal footing

In some cities, there may be one other indirect way for funders to reinforce charter schools. They can support the movement to create Collaboration Compacts between school districts and charter schools. Led by the Bill & Melinda Gates Foundation, this is an effort to bring together political leaders, different school operators, and community stakeholders in a region to hammer out agreements for sharing ideas, buildings, teacher training, enrollment systems, measurement tests, and other resources among different types of schools.

This is not strictly charter school work—the Compacts simply aim to make it as easy as possible for families in particular neighborhoods to get good schooling, with the idea that authorities should be more agnostic than in the past about what sector a child is instructed in—conventional school, charter school, or parochial school. But of course putting charters on an "equal" footing with conventional schools (and in Boston and Philadelphia including parochial schools in the mix as well!) is itself quite a victory for supporters of educational alternatives that have long been relegated to step-child status.

Gates recently granted $25 million to seven cities to cement their "Compacts." Some seem more successful than others. In Philadelphia (where public education has been riven with dissension), the Compact is being administered by a group called the Philadelphia School Partnership that aims to shift local focus toward the quality of instruction that children get rather than what kind of school it takes place in. The Partnership includes any school that serves primarily low-income kids—which deals 85 charter schools (educating 26 percent of Philly's kids) plus all

> The charter school revolution has only begun to unfold on a mass level. There remain many opportunities for donors to be leaders.

of the Catholic archdiocese schools into the mix. Partnership resources are being shared, and additional outside funders are being rallied to supplement funds beyond the $2.5 million Gates has already awarded. The money will be used for things like building a common website where parents can compare and select schools from a single entry point.

How successful this effort will be in bringing peace and better performance to public schooling remains to be seen. At least rhetorically, though, this is the charter school dream: the educational establishment becoming even-handed about school structure, and focusing instead on who gets the best results. With Gates leadership and financial support, 16 cities are currently experimenting with Compacts, including New York City, Denver, Boston, Hartford, and New Orleans. It is possible that as schools begin to cope with the new Common Core requirements now unfolding across the U.S. this kind of educational détente and collaboration could increase. Philanthropists will want to keep an eye on this development and consider adding their impetus if the Compact strategy shows promise in one of their target cities.

Other kinds of support: advocacy, business aid, data systems

In addition to funding charter school incubators, philanthropists can make it easier for charters to thrive by supporting charter school advocacy groups in their states. These groups chip away at policy issues that are important to charters, often easing the task of school creation in the process. Chapter 5 of this book looks in depth at the need for advocacy, but to give an indication of how this kind of work can fuel school growth, here are a few examples of the kinds of tasks that today's donor-supported advocacy groups help charters with:

- Lobbying state legislators to allow equitable funding for charter schools. (Most states reimburse charters at a much lower rate per enrolled student than they pay conventional schools. There is no fair justification for this; underfunding of charters was just one of the ways that opponents were appeased when charter laws were first voted on.)
- Encouraging regulators to help charters find and pay for buildings. (Many states currently provide no facilities funding, only paying for instructional expenses once the school is already set up. Needless to say this makes life difficult for many school founders.)
- Resisting efforts by opponents to stifle charter schools by capping their allowed numbers at some arbitrary low level. (Even in states where cramping caps have been imposed, charter school advocates have sometimes been able to convince officials to exempt charter schools that demonstrate superior results, creating some wiggle room for serving additional children.)

Another way donors can strengthen charter school numbers is by bolstering the internal operations of extant, successful operators. The Tiger Foundation, Broad Foundation, Fisher Fund, NewSchools Venture Fund, Charter School Growth Fund, and other givers have supported the central offices of multi-school charter operators by providing grants that enable them to build their organizations. Sometimes these support the hiring of senior staff members, or contracts with outside experts who handle finance, human resources, business planning, or the data systems used to assess students, teachers, and schools. Other times the grants pay for long-term planning, or help develop the internal capacity of these operators to manage more campuses. Many philanthropists have provided general operating support to the top nonprofit charter operators, in the belief that strengthening these enterprises who have already proven themselves is the best way to bring the benefits of charter schools to more of the hundreds of thousands of children aching to attend but lacking a space.

There are also intermediaries across the country, very deserving of philanthropic support, that bolster charter schools from within. These provide on-site support to keep extant schools academically strong and financially healthy. They provide networks and meetings with peers where charter school leaders can learn from each other. They offer continuous training and leadership development to educators. You'll be introduced to scores of these groups in the course of this book.

The Michael & Susan Dell Foundation has been an important backer of intermediary organizations that bolster the charter movement broadly. They have built support organizations at both the state and national level to help charter schools maintain their independence and excellence. The California Charter Schools Association and the Texas Charter Schools Association have both been important beneficiaries of Dell support.

A special effort of the foundation has been to encourage meaningful definitions of quality, and to demand self-policing within charter groups in order to keep standards high. Dell has helped fund customizable training programs that hundreds of schools in these trade groups have used to improve the skills of their teachers and administrators. Paying for online data-sharing platforms where schools publish their results has been another practical contribution.

Honest and rigorous measurement of school outcomes is a deep interest of Dell. Having invested tens of millions of dollars in charter schools over the last decade or so, the foundation has found that management can get trickier, and academic performance less consistent, when an organization expands to five or more schools. After uncovering this common tipping point the foundation began to complement its expansion funding with support for strong performance-management systems that help educators monitor and maintain their quality across an entire portfolio of schools.

Dell staffers also developed a tool for screening current and potential grantees. This assessment program factors in student-achievement results, leadership capability, and resource management. It generates performance comparisons to surrounding schools, to other charter operators, to different regions. This helps the foundation identify areas of strength and challenge, zero in on best practices, and target their funding.

Good data helps Dell program officers provide valuable feedback to school operators. They report that educators find it particularly useful to see their performance compared in detail to other high-performing charter organizations from other places. Central headquarters expenditures across different charter networks are the kind of information that operators would otherwise find very hard to assess.

Dell's analytical tools make it easier to see how many of the charter schools they fund are improving their performance from year to year. The foundation likes to compare networks not only to their previous years' results but also to surrounding schools in their host district. It is partly the power of their statistical tools that has allowed the Michael & Susan Dell Foundation to zero their grantmaking in on charters capable of strong annual performance growth—often double-digit rises in recent data.

Lots of opportunities to act

The nearly 7,000 charter schools that have been formed from scratch over the last two decades represent one of the great self-organizing social movements of our age. It is an independent citizen response to heartbreaking educational failures that the responsible public institutions showed no capacity to solve on their own. And nearly all of the innovation was powered by philanthropy.

Yet even as charter schooling matures as a philanthropic field, there remain many opportunities for donors to be leaders, and even pathbreakers. The charter school revolution has only begun to unfold on a mass level. Wise donors will choose their path carefully. Do you want to create new school models? Do you want to clone the best of existing schools? Would you rather work on improving average schools? Maybe pushing for the closure of poor schools is where you can best make your mark. You could combine two or more of these efforts, or concentrate on one. Think and plan how you can have the greatest effect in your area.

By inventing new schools, reproducing high-quality existing schools, and supporting myriad intermediary organizations that bolster charter schooling, funders have already changed the lives of millions of under-provided children. Nearly three million American youngsters will attend charter schools in the next school season, and the number climbs fast every year. Given the extent to which demand for charters among families currently outstrips supply, continuing to open new high-performing schools will remain a powerful imperative for the foreseeable future.

As inspired education reformers and their allies in American civil society open the country's next 7,000 charter schools, the other challenge for donors will be to keep a close eye on quality controls, on the supply of talented teachers and principals, and on the government policies that speed or block school success. Each of these factors will be addressed in subsequent chapters.

Improving School Quality and Accountability

As charter schools continue to multiply, they are becoming the dominant competitor to conventional district schools. Already, charter school students are more numerous than students in Catholic schools, other religious schools, or homeschooling (each of which hosts something under 2 million students), and they are three times as numerous as students in private secular schools (900,000). Within a decade, there may be as many American children in charter schools as in all of these other alternatives to conventional public school *combined*. Charters will be U.S. education's leading Plan B.

In this ever-more-popular, multimillion-student world, maintaining the quality of charter schools will be essential. "The challenge is increasingly to keep an eye on performance," says Kevin Hall of the Charter School Growth Fund, "and to ensure that we take aggressive action when quality is not as high as it needs to be."

Maintaining elevated standards among charters is important to the children who attend them today. It's also important to protecting the public reputation of charters so they can continue to expand as alternatives to conventional schools. In a world where opponents of charters will to be quick to pounce on every weak result, charter supporters need to be demanding and enforce high expectations, so that the overall system generates excitement and support, allowing more children to have choices in the future.

One way that funders can assist in weeding out weak charters and keeping quality up is to create good measurement systems that assess how well schools are doing, and then get their results into the hands of authorizers and the general public in easily understood forms. By supplying families and authorizers with clear information on the performance of their local schools, donors can enable careful and accurate decisions. Being schools of choice, the users of charters can walk away if results droop. Charters have no captive audience.

Another method for bolstering charter school quality is to improve the authorizing system. It is authorizers in each state or city who select, monitor, and close charter schools. The education experts surveyed for this book by The Philanthropy Roundtable were asked to identify the greatest weaknesses of the charter movement throughout the past five years. Fully 98 percent picked "limited authorizer accountability for student results," and 93 percent selected "failure to close enough low-quality schools."

Whether it happens via families voting with their feet or authorizing officials pronouncing with their pens, culling out weak performers is a healthy process. Donor Katherine Bradley, who has helped drive D.C.'s charter successes, notes that protecting schools from stiff market tests does our education system no favor. "Pressure to the system can actually be good. Our job as guardians is to keep pushing things. Let the resultant stress and change happen, and build a system where schools are adapting and getting better in the face of stressors. Some won't make it, and that's okay. Other schools will rise to these market demands."

Tougher authorizing

Charter school authorizers—the agencies that dispense charters and hold schools accountable—are supposed to be responsible for screening out poorly prepared applicants, overseeing schools, reviewing results, reinforcing schools that are lagging, and then closing down those that still fail their students. The researchers behind the 2013 Stanford CREDO study are blunt: "The quality of the charter sector at any point in time is largely determined by who is permitted to obtain a charter."

Fully 90 percent of all authorizers today are local school districts. The remaining 10 percent of authorizers, though, are much more active and launch far more schools each, on average. So if you count

> The charter sector as a whole has been too soft on getting rid of low performers.

the schools rather than the authorizers, you find that while 52 percent of all charter schools got their license to practice from a local district, the other half were authorized by a state education agency (19 percent of all schools), an independent board created specifically to authorize charter schools (15 percent), a college (9 percent), a nonprofit organization (4 percent), or a mayor or city council (less than 1 percent of all charter schools).

If authorizers quail or fail at their duties, quality can suffer fast. According to James Shelton, a former program director for education at the Bill & Melinda Gates Foundation who is currently a high official in the U.S. Department of Education, "the Achilles Heel of the charter school movement has been governance. The charter sector as a whole has been too soft on getting rid of low performers."

Authorizers need intellectual, financial, technical, and moral support from donors that encourages them to make hard choices. Closing low-performing schools is tricky. There can be legal action to contest decisions. Impassioned community protests are common. Accommodating students who are displaced by closures can be tough.

To help local authorities better navigate both the front-end quality screens and the back-end closure process, the National Association of Charter School Authorizers published an "Index of Essential Practices" in 2012. It grades member authorizers on their adherence to 12 fundamental indicators of quality. NACSA also holds a national conference for authorizers, promulgates regularly updated best practices in authorizing, conducts training for authorizers, provides in-depth assistance to authorizers who end up in a pickle, and speaks for its members in policy circles.

There is plenty of room for more such guidance. Donors who want to improve authorizing could help by shedding light on current policies and practices, and by encouraging and supporting parties who are trying to build up the intellectual underpinnings and managerial strengths of authorizers.

Philanthropists wishing to make a mark on local authorizing practices might follow the lead of the Annie E. Casey Foundation. Casey provided multi-year support to help then-mayor Bart Peterson develop a top-notch authorizing system in Indianapolis. The grants enabled the mayor's office to design a rigorous application process, a thorough results-based accountability system, and a web portal providing information to families. After being launched with philanthropic dollars, the office is now self-sustaining. Similarly, the Doris & Donald Fisher Fund provided resources to help California's authorizers improve the processes they use to vet applications, via a grant funneled through NACSA. Many other authorizers could similarly strengthen their operations if offered such assistance.

One of the most effective authorizing bodies in the country today is the Public Charter School Board of the District of Columbia (where 43 percent of all the children who attend public schools are in charters and an additional 27 percent of the population is pounding on the door from a charter waiting list). It took the district a while to get its charter system on track. In the beginning, the old, politicized board of education was also an authorizer, and lots of mediocre schools got approved. But today the PCSB (whose members are appointed by the mayor and confirmed by the city council) is D.C.'s only charter authorizer, and it relies on detailed rating systems both to assess new applications and to track school quality once campuses are open.

The PCSB has created what it calls its "performance management framework" to assess various elements of academic progress and school climate so that different schools can be compared in a consistent way. Schools get scored on a scale from zero to 100, and the performance reports are made available to the public through an open website. The highest-performing schools receive less frequent monitoring from the board and are encouraged to expand their programs and open new campuses.

The board offers schools that receive weak scores a few semesters to improve and move up the rating scale. If they don't, those facilities are closed. Unlike in some places, this is not an idle possibility. The list of D.C. charter schools that have been shuttered now numbers 41, with the four latest closures taking place in 2013. All were penalized for academic weakness.

"When you close low performers you thereby create space for new innovators to come in and try new models," explains Brian Jones, chairman of the board when these latest charters were pulled. "Part of the genius of the charter model is it does allow for a certain innovative churn," Jones told the *Washington Post*.

The particular ways the PCSB handled these latest closures offer a glimpse into the sophistication of the organization's operations. One of the unsuccessful schools was required to shutter two of its three campuses and to surrender its right to operate grades 1-8, but it was allowed to use its third campus to focus on early childhood education. A different underperforming school was required to relinquish its charter, but the board allowed a merger of some of the school's assets, plus its student body, into another charter school. This was a first for the board, an experiment aimed at helping the families caught up in the shutdown find replacement seats for their children. (The students will shift to a more effective Achievement Prep charter.) Meanwhile, another low-performing school will be given several months to improve its student outcomes; if it fails, the campus will either be closed or perhaps merged with a better functioning school along the lines of the Achievement Prep example.

Like charter schools themselves, the best charter authorizers are innovating in entrepreneurial ways, with a strong focus on demonstrated performance, but a willingness to entertain unconventional ways of achieving that. And unsentimental toughness is as necessary in the initial authorizing process as it is for closures. The D.C. Public Charter School Board requires applicants for new charters to provide extensive detail on precisely how they will measure and improve the performance of their students—and it is picky. In 2013, the board received nine applications for new charters. It approved only two. "You want a system that is loose enough to allow innovation but also has a high bar for approval and takes closure seriously," is how the board's executive director, Scott Pearson, explained their process to the *Wall Street Journal*.

Donors emphasize school quality

Private donors have been crucial in raising performance standards within the charter sector. In the early days, the focus of charter advocates—and many donors—was on rapidly expanding the number of schools. Expansion is still a priority, but most funders now insist that the schools they back must be able to show superior student results, compared to other institutions with similar student bodies. This has taken on real urgency with the most active donors.

Despite widespread agreement that school quality is important, opinions have sometimes conflicted on the question of what exactly "quality" means. With the aim of developing agreement on the specific elements a charter school should have in order to be considered a success, a group of donors backed a project called Building Charter School Quality. The Michael & Susan Dell Foundation, the Gates Foundation, and the Annie E. Casey Foundation were lead funders. The project convened education reformers, nonprofit leaders, academics, regulators, and foundations, and hammered out two reports, *A Framework for Academic Quality* and *A Framework for Operational Quality*, that set baselines for the intellectual and managerial measures that should be used to define quality charter schools.

The National Association of Charter School Authorizers took the work of the consortium to the next level by providing assistance to partners needing to adapt the standards to particular populations (like special-needs schools). NACSA has also been heavily involved in defining quality when it comes to the process of charter school authorizing itself. Every year, the group publishes updated standards for what a good charter school authorizer should look for, centered around three core principles: maintaining high standards, upholding school

> Thanks to donors, the website GreatSchools.org provides information on the quality of thousands of schools (district, charter, religious, private alike) on an easily used, ad-supported site.

autonomy, and protecting student and public interests. This material is available at qualitycharters.org.

The Walton Family Foundation provided funds to help NACSA focus its membership on taking *action* once these quality standards are in place. Guidelines were created on the specifics of how poor and mediocre charter schools can either be improved, transferred to new management, or shut down. After all, standards are only relevant if there are consequential actions when they are breached.

Donors who fund schools directly must have their own basic tests of what constitutes an excellent institution. Some apply the rule of thumb that a very good school should average 1.5 years of learning growth in one school year when its students take annual assessments. It is not uncommon for top charters to test out at that exemplary level (see "What exactly does the latest research say about charter quality?" on page 65).

The Michael & Susan Dell Foundation has labored to establish detailed quality definitions for use in its own charter school grantmaking. The foundation offers what it calls performance-management grants to help schools collect detailed data on how well they are hitting their targets. The foundation's "Ed-Fi" software platform pulls together in one place all of the statistics on a particular school's performance, standardizes them for comparison to other institutions, then puts the results on a website available not only to the foundation but also to teachers and leaders at its recipient schools so they can use the information in their decisionmaking.

Results can be aggregated for a whole city, or for other schools in different cities but the same management network. The system is designed to be used without needing extra staff, so that even cash-strapped institutions without an IT department can use it. Dell would like to see Ed-Fi used widely to "supplement or replace measures used for broader state or federal accountability reporting," and makes the tool available for all to use with a free license.

Putting money behind report cards

Some donors are investing in third-party services that shine bright lights on student outcomes—making it easy for any observer to see where children are learning, and where they aren't. For instance, a number of foundations—Gates, Robertson, Arnold, Walton, Schwab, Packard, Joyce, Kern, Bradley, and others—paid for construction of the website Great-Schools.org, which provides information on the quality of thousands of schools (district, charter, religious, private alike) on an easily used, ad-supported site. "Families looking for better choices need more of this kind of easily digested information," suggests Bruno Manno of the Walton Family Foundation. "It would be useful for philanthropists to fund local variants of Great Schools that are even more detailed, to match the needs of today's kids with the schools that currently exist."

There are opportunities for funders to contribute to national, state, or local information platforms like these. For example, the Philadelphia School Partnership produces a website and print publication entitled "Great Philly Schools" that provides performance data on every campus in the city—district, charter, parochial, and private. "Parents are hungry for this information," says Mark Gleason, executive director of the organization. "In less than a year, we've had more than 50,000 hits on the Great Philly Schools website, and in three weeks, we exhausted our supply of 45,000 print editions."

Many states now offer report cards on all of their public schools—including charters—often with philanthropic help. In Connecticut, for example, ConnCAN is a donor-driven 501(c)(3) with more than a dozen staff that provides parents and interested citizens with individual school profiles (at reportcards.conncan.org), along with research on education reform, aids to school advocacy, and lots of energy on behalf of school excellence. A mix of 156 individual donors and 27 foundations or corporations (including the Robertson, William E. Simon, Steven and Alexandra Cohen, and Bodman foundations) funded the center in its latest year.

In addition to supporting efforts that rate individual schools, donors can create and share information on how charter schools are performing as a sector. The Boston Foundation made a strategic investment a few years ago in a 2009 study, and then a 2010 update, in which scholars from Harvard, MIT, Michigan, and Duke universities compared student achievement at charter schools in Boston with the city's other public schools. These found that the charter schools perform significantly better. The study was carefully designed to factor out or equalize influences like student background and parental motivation, so its results made quite an impression.

At about the same time, a clutch of donors banded together to commission some bold charter school research covering the nation as a whole, along with communications mechanisms to transmit the findings to interested parties. The Achelis & Bodman Foundations, the Heinz Endowments, the Rodel Charitable Trust, the Annie E. Casey

Foundation, the Daniels Fund, the Fisher Fund, the Fordham Foundation, the Gates Foundation, the Ewing Marion Kauffman Foundation, and the Walton Family Foundation provided funds which allowed the University of Washington's Center on Reinventing Public Education to create a string of publications. CRPE's landmark 2011 study *The Effect of Charter Schools on Student Achievement* had pulled together the whole charter school literature to that point and conducted sophisticated data analysis. The overall finding was that charter schools were outperforming conventional public schools with similar student bodies, and outpacing other popular school reforms like reducing class size.

Many smart donors helped the National Alliance for Public Charter Schools create, throughout a decade, a more-or-less annual report called *Measuring Charter Performance,* which summarized what hundreds of academic studies were finding about the effects of charter schools. In April 2013, the Alliance created a more succinct and easier-to-digest summary—still drawing from the best recent research studies, but aimed at a wider audience—entitled *Public Charter School Success.* It gathers together much striking evidence that charter schools are having good outcomes. Funding was provided by prominent ed-reform philanthropists, including the Fisher Fund, the Carnegie Corporation, and the Arnold, Gates, Kauffman, Kern, Robertson, Schwab, Simon, and Walton foundations.

What exactly does the latest research say about charter quality? The Robertson Foundation, established by financier Julian Robertson and family, has helped tighten quality within the charter school universe by paying for careful evaluations. They funded the 2013 CREDO study (summarized in Chapter 1, and further discussed later in this chapter) that has been so important in helping observers understand which charter schools are succeeding.

Additional funding from Robertson plus money from the Fairbanks and Smith Richardson foundations and others allowed the CREDO researchers to go beyond their national summary and produce region-specific analyses of charter school performance. During 2012 and 2013, they conducted quality studies in five states. The findings are helping local donors (of which the Robertson Foundation is one—they helped build the New York City Center for Charter School Excellence, and have supported the expansion of excellent charter schools within that city) refine the performance of their surrounding charters.

The CREDO regional results suggest how high the bar has risen in the charter sector.

- In Massachusetts, the typical charter school student now absorbs the equivalent of two and a half extra months of math learning every year compared to peers in public schools, and one and a half extra months in reading. This advantage was even larger at big city schools. In Boston, charter students surpassed conventional school students by the equivalent of 13 months of additional learning per year in math, and 12 additional months in reading. In other words, by the time regular public school kids learned one year of material, the charter pupils had absorbed about two years worth of knowledge. Fully 83 percent of all Boston charter schools showed bigger learning gains than their district school counterparts. Not one single Boston charter school was found to have significantly lower than average learning gains.
- In Michigan, the Stanford researchers found, a typical charter school student gained an extra two months of learning in both math and reading over the course of a school year, compared to regular public school children. Here again, the advantage was especially pronounced within urban areas, where charter kids gained nearly three months of extra achievement. In math, 42 percent of Michigan charter schools outperformed their district school counterparts, with only 6 percent performing worse. In reading, 35 percent exceeded district schools, while 2 percent lagged.
- The same investigation in New York City found charter school students outstripping others by five months of extra learning per year in math, and one extra month in reading.
- Indiana students absorbed an extra month and a half of learning per year in both math and reading.
- And in New Jersey, charter students gained three extra months of learning in math, and two extra months in reading, each school year. The big-city effect was again present: in Newark, charter students gained an additional nine months per year in math, and seven and a half months in reading.

The year 2013 produced a statewide study from Florida as well, conducted by the State Department of Education. It found that charter schools had a higher percentage of students scoring at grade level or better in the annual statewide math and reading tests. In addition, the statewide achievement lags of African-American, Hispanic, other non-English speakers, and low-income students were reduced in charter schools.

A major study of results in the charter schools operated all across the nation by KIPP (by far today's largest nonprofit charter school operator) was also released in 2013. This again was a high-quality investigation, conducted by social scientists at Mathematica Policy Research. The findings:

- In math, a typical student who spends three years in a KIPP charter school will absorb 11 months of extra learning compared to where he or she would have ended up without KIPP
- In reading, the average result was eight additional months of learning
- In science, KIPP schools produced the equivalent of 14 months of extra learning
- In social studies, the KIPP bonus was 11 months' worth of learning

The common perception that charter schools produce results not much different from conventional schools is an inaccuracy based on old research, describing the earliest charter schools rather than the more evolved and much more effective schools that are now being replicated in large number. The research summary in 2013's *Public Charter School Success* encapsulates the most recent academic findings this way:

> Three national studies and ten studies from major regions across the country since 2010 found positive academic performance results for students in public charter schools compared to their traditional public school peers.... As the public charter sector matures, charter school leaders...are increasingly focusing their attention on school quality. The achievement studies suggest that the focus on quality is producing results.

Publicizing up-to-date performance research is one way donors could bring more clarity and discerning action to the question of charter quality.

Closure: The case for pruning the charter school orchard

"While many success stories reveal the potential of high-quality charter schools, there are also plenty of poorly performing charters. It is important that those schools be closed," states Kevin Hall of the Charter School Growth Fund without hedging. "That protects the integrity of the charter school proposition: increased flexibility in exchange for performance accountability."

Barbara Hyde, who has been a major funder of successful charter schools in Memphis, Tennessee, and elsewhere, insists that "we philanthropists have an obligation to model for districts what districts don't do—and that is close down schools that aren't performing. The charter school movement needs to be quick in identifying schools that are the lowest performing, intervene when we can, but then shut them down if there's no improvement. Because that's what the public schools need to learn to do. If we can't model that ourselves, then we're not teaching the systems what they need to learn."

Don't assume that school users will automatically recognize and foreclose on lagging academic quality. Lots of things go into a family's choice of schools. Safety, convenience of location, shiny facilities, neighborhood familiarity, sports, and other factors can sometimes mask poor academic results. In some ways it's natural for children and families to become complacent about a school once they have settled into it. The personnel and routines become comfortable. You lose any sense of what other students in other places are learning, and how you might rank.

And of course any school change can seem scary or disruptive, so inertia often favors the status quo. Even if you develop a suspicion that your local school is not delivering as it should, the prospect of seeing teachers let go, or a principal turned over, or even maybe having the facility shut down, can leave some parents more worried about disruptions than excited about new possibilities. Even the friskiest aspirations to seek a better education can be damped by the possibility of a new bus trip across town, a substantial expenditure of cash, or a wrenching home move. No wonder there is often a tendency to turn a blind eye when schools disappoint academically.

Conventional public schools are almost impossible to shut down, repopulate with fresh teachers, or reorient in any fundamental way, so they almost demand fatalistic acceptance. But why should the stakeholders in charter schools accept mediocre and sclerotic performance? The whole charter ethic—extra freedom in exchange for extra performance—argues that when a weak performer appears, it should be energetically amended, and eventually lose its license if that doesn't help. The question is whether authorizers will be willing to drop the hammer, and whether donors, parents, and other interested parties will help them make the tough choices.

In the 2012-2013 school year, there were 561 new charter schools opened. In the same year, 206 were closed down (out of a national total of 6,004 charter schools). Closures are not the only form of discipline in the system—other low-quality schools were required to merge or reorganize. Nonetheless, that 3 percent annual rate of turning out the lights on laggards is probably not enough.

The landmark Stanford CREDO study of charter school quality offers interesting discussion on the closing of low-performing schools as a strategy for improving overall quality. The researchers include five possible "closure scenarios" in their report. The mildest option involves shutting down schools that don't produce a minimum level of academic growth among their students; this would axe about 170 existing charter schools nationwide. Another of the CREDO scenarios would shut down the lowest 10 percent of all charter schools by average achievement level. That would mean closing about 680 schools. Their high-end possibility would be to pull charters from schools that shows less academic growth than some traditional public school in its local area—this would eliminate about 1,700 schools.

There would obviously be dislocations involved in closing schools like this, but "closure" doesn't have to mean the school gets padlocked or students stranded. Typically, pupils are redirected to a better-performing school nearby. Sometimes new operators take over the existing building and student body. The management and instructional team get closed down, but a range of transition options exists.

The Stanford study shows, however, that shutting down the sector's weak performers in any of these ways would have clear and immediate positive results. It would raise the achievement of U.S. students, and improve the net effectiveness of charter schools. The

> The whole charter ethic—extra freedom in exchange for extra performance—argues that when a weak performer appears, it should be energetically amended.

more bottom-dwellers that get replaced with an average or better charter, the more positive the effect on total student achievement.

A 2013 analysis by the Fordham Institute and Public Impact showed that strategic closures could bring dramatic improvement to the charter sector. The study included a simulation of the impact of closing the lowest-performing 10 percent of charter schools in five select cities, while replicating the top performers in those cities by an equal percentage. The simulation for Cleveland, for example, found that this approach would lead to charter schools in the city substantially outperforming their district peers. In fact, within five years of such a strategic pruning, the performance of inner-city students in Cleveland charters would match the average achievement of all students in the state of Ohio (there is currently no place in America where inner-city students exceed statewide performance averages).

Unsentimentally closing low-performing charters and shifting their students to high performers of the type we now know how to replicate would bring dramatic payoffs. For that reason, the nonprofit that represents charter granting entities—the National Association of Charter School Authorizers—is now on record in support of tough closure rates. NACSA has suggested that shuttering 1,000 of the nation's poorest performing charters would be good for the charter school movement and students alike.

A school closure strategy that would dramatically improve any city

Of course, shuttering several thousand of the poorest performing *conventional* public schools would also be great for the nation, but the lack of any accountability mechanism for those campuses lets them fumble along indefinitely. Neerav Kingsland, one of the chief architects of the charter school revolution in New Orleans, has a crisp strategy for deploying closure to improve public education generally. By following the same plan he is pursuing in New Orleans (with widespread donor support), any city can raise its average student achievement while simultaneously building a high-quality charter network.

Every year, Kingsland suggests, education authorities should shut down the weakest 5 percent of schools in their city. Whether they are conventional schools or charter schools doesn't matter—whichever schools do least to raise the performance of their pupils should get axed. Simultaneously, new charters should be offered to a sufficient number of quality operators to replace the seats eliminated. Any city that followed this strategy over a five-year period would thus replace the wobbliest 25 percent of its campuses with higher-performing institutions, while building a solid critical mass of effective charter schools.

To give you a sense of what this would require as a practical matter, a large city like Chicago would need to close about 34 weak schools every year, and then replace them with 34 carefully chartered new schools. A smaller city like Newark would have to close and replace four poor schools each year. Is this doable?

Yes, says Kingsland. First you build a state or local accountability system that allows schools to be compared on an apples-to-apples basis, so the bottom 5 percent can be clearly identified. Then, he suggests, create a new nonprofit or government entity with authority to take over the failing schools and close them, while authorizing new charter schools to take their places. "This will give you the pressure and cover you need to be aggressive," he counsels local school reformers. And the end result? Citywide academic performance will rise crisply, and students will be much better served.

Even cities too disorganized or divided to close down their low-quality conventional schools as Kingsland suggests should at least be sure they annually pare out their weak charter schools. The fact that charters have a regular, built-in thumbs-up or thumbs-down renewal process is one of their great advantages. Failing to bravely exercise the option would undercut one of the biggest advantages charter schools offer a community.

The record on this front has been uneven in recent years. According to one NACSA study, more than 12 percent of all charter schools that came up for renewal back in the 2008-2009 school year were denied a fresh authorization. More recently, that figure fell to 6 percent.

One might argue that this decline partly reflects the fact that fewer weak new schools are coming on line as the charter sector matures. Ten years ago, fully two thirds of all applications for new charters were approved. Today, scrutiny is tighter, and only about one third of all applications get approved. The largest number of new charter schools opening these days are replications of clearly successful "franchises" like KIPP, Uncommon Schools, Achievement First, YES Prep, Green Dot, Great Hearts, BASIS, Rocketship, and so forth, almost all of which will produce strong results for their students.

But there remains a powerful argument for shutting down existing mediocrities. Remember that one of the more fascinating findings in

Stanford's CREDO study was that overall student results in the charter sector are improving not because existing schools are getting dramatically better, but because 1) more and more of the proven high-performing schools are being opened every year, and 2) underperforming schools are being shut down. While the 2009 version of the CREDO study found charter schools as a group performing slightly below other schools, the 2013 update found charter schools as a group had moved above their competitors in test results. And a major factor driving this shift up the performance curve was the fact that 8 percent of the schools that were underperforming in 2009 got closed down by authorizers.

This suggests that philanthropists should exercise a tough love in their giving, and encourage their area's state and city authorizers to be equally serious. We now know the importance of intervening quickly in schools that disappoint in their early years. The CREDO research demonstrates that 80 percent of schools that are low-performing during their first year are still low-performing five years later. (Meanwhile, 94 percent of the schools that start out great in their first year remain great.) The data say that a school which begins with an ineffective formula is highly unlikely to improve, so delaying interventions and then sanctions only penalizes the enrolled children.

"Holding high standards will be essential to achieving success as charter schools grow," says Janet Mountain, executive director of the Michael & Susan Dell Foundation. "If we pursue growth without penalizing disappointing results, the kind of sclerosis, bureaucracy, and declining academic results we see in other parts of public schooling will be a risk."

Jed Wallace of the California Charter School Association underlines the point. "We need significantly better learning opportunities than are available within conventional schools. That means not only supporting the growth of high-performing charter schools, but also shining a light on those that are not providing good quality. In doing so we reaffirm the accountability that parents and the public wish to see in place for all public schools."

Philanthropists should exercise a tough love in their giving, and encourage their area's authorizers to be equally serious in dealing with disappointing schools.

Lessons from a funder turned authorizer

The Thomas B. Fordham Foundation was an early and enthusiastic backer of charter schools, and remains one to this day. In 2005, it took its support in a new direction. Fordham became a licensed charter school authorizer in the state of Ohio, responsible for approving and then assuring the quality of the charter schools under its jurisdiction. Here is Fordham president Chester Finn's summary of what his foundation learned by assuming an inside position in the authorization process:

> Like many sponsors, we inherited a bevy of already established charters. Without us, they would have been orphaned—and maybe died. We thought we scrutinized these charter schools carefully before taking them on, but we weren't careful enough. We didn't appreciate the extent to which they would arrive with their own idiosyncrasies, bad habits, and settled governance and staffing arrangements. Sometimes these proved to be strengths, but too often turned out to be frailties.
>
> Though we've wanted to open new schools, we labor under state-imposed "caps" that make it exceedingly difficult. Worse, our state's school-funding structure makes it hard for charter operators to make ends meet. And the charter program in Ohio has been under constant attack by critics. When they fail with the legislature, they turn to the courts, the media, local government—anything they can do to create hassles for authorizers and charter schools.
>
> A lot of time and effort has had to be spent on complying with authorizer requirements (processing forms, making reports, etc.) while also making sure our schools fulfill innumerable laws and regulations. Ohio's charter laws resemble an archeological dig in Jericho, with layer upon layer of frequently conflicting rules, expectations, and procedures. Many dollars have been spent on attorney fees.
>
> With more than 60 authorizers in Ohio, there are some perverse incentives for schools to seek out the sponsor that will create the fewest hassles and charge the lowest fees. Though we could be "fired" by the Ohio Department of Education, many other authorizers have a statutory "right," grandfathered in legislation, to sponsor schools indefinitely, be those schools good, bad, or indifferent.

One of the most useful things an authorizer can do is to close an ineffective school and replace it with a better one. In 2013, about 35,000 charter students in Ohio attended charter schools that got Ds or Fs from the state on achievement and growth. My ballpark estimate is that a quarter to a third of all charter students in our state are attending schools that cannot be justified. (Of course the same is true of many district schools.)

It is, however, often vexing and difficult to carry off a closure. Some schools that face closure are run by earnest, decent people for incredibly needy kids in areas where the other schools are awful. The two schools where we faced closing were really inadequate, yet nevertheless the best in their neighborhood! They didn't meet our standards, and we were repeatedly investing time and money in trying to get the people running them to function better. We failed over and over.

The doctrine says close that school. But the reality is it can be hard. At least the school is safe; the students are learning a little. Closing the doors could put 322 kids in worse schools, at least in the short term. Closure is also a political problem with the community. In the end, we terminated our authorizing relationship with those two schools, because they couldn't meet our standards. But another authorizer picked up overseeing them, and they didn't close.

One thing we and other authorizers would welcome help with is an impartial, external review when a decision has to be made about closing a school. We'd love to bring in a dispassionate team of experts to spend a few days going over the school with a fine-tooth comb. That can easily be a $10,000 or $20,000 investment, which many authorizers can't afford. Yet it would really help in cases where dramatic intervention is being considered.

The first thing to do would be a diagnostic, "Can this school be cured?" If a school is really misfiring, there is cover for action. This is something funders could help excellent authorizers do.

Fresh eyes can be valuable not just for overall judgment, but also for technical assistance. The site-visit team might help the school find a consultant. Help them outsource their back office if it's the business management that's bad. Help them find a curriculum expert if that's screwed up. Help them with staff development.

But almost all these things cost money. Philanthropic dollars could jump start some authorizers to the next level by giving them the kind of capacities I've just described.

Donors should also make sure that when new authorizers are set up they get strong capabilities from the beginning. I believe when Colorado finally established a statewide authorizer, the legislature initially didn't appropriate a single dollar to pay for it. So for the first year or two philanthropy got them on their feet.

Bringing Top Teachers and Principals to Charters

What makes a school good? Is it bright classrooms, modern labs, and spacious facilities? Small group instruction? A rich curriculum? Up-to-date technology? Strong administrators? Those things are all nice, but the research is clear that none are overwhelmingly important to student outcomes. What *is* important—two to three times as important as any other school factor—is the quality of the institution's teachers.

(It's sobering to note that one other influence makes even teacher quality pale in significance: the family status and background of a child may have four to eight times as much impact on student achievement as the level of teaching, according to RAND Corporation investigators. But family breakdown is a problem for another book. Schools must work with what comes in the door, and when it comes to remediation the biggest lever we can pull is the excellence of our teachers.)

The studies on what goes into teacher excellence are quite specific. Factors often assumed to be synonymous with the quality of educating—like master's degrees and other paper credentials, state licensing, being on the job a long time, low class size, teacher salaries, and overall spending on education—turn out to matter not so much. Two factors that do matter: the instructor's specific content knowledge, and his or her general intelligence.

That's the verdict not only of academic research but also of field practice. "The number-one thing schools can do to unlock the potential of their students is to give them great teachers," says Ariela Rozman, CEO of the teacher-training nonprofit TNTP. "Our teachers are everything," says Michael Block, who leads BASIS, one of the most effective charter school networks in the country. "They know and love their content, and everything flows from that."

Block's mention of content is crucial. Many conventional public schools are not allowed to hire mathematicians to teach math, or people who've written books to lead students through literature. State policies generally require graduates of teaching colleges, most of whose training is in education theory and pedagogy, not subject matter. "Teacher preparation programs are too heavily weighted with courses in educational methods at the expense of courses in subjects to be taught," warned the National Commission on Excellence in Education as far back as 1983.

Many charter schools are a reaction against this old style of teacher credentialing. "We look for content expertise first and foremost," explains Craig Barrett, the former Intel CEO who went on to fund and guide the creation of BASIS Schools, making sure that retired engineers and professional musicians and history Ph.D.s would be welcome in its classrooms even if they lacked a degree from a teaching college. The philosophy at BASIS, and many other top charter schools, is that "all teachers should be content experts in the fields they are teaching. You can't do a good job teaching kids math unless you know and love math, nor English, nor history, nor science," says Barrett.

There is evidence backing this approach. Multiple studies find that teachers who hold a degree in mathematics (as opposed to a general teaching degree) are associated with higher student math scores, that teachers with strong training in other disciplines will inculcate more knowledge of that discipline in their pupils. The recommendation of the Carnegie Foundation for the Advancement of Teaching is that all teachers ought to complete four years of courses in an established academic major, and then spend a fifth year learning about education methods. Other advisory groups have likewise suggested that colleges training teachers should first require a standard baccalaureate degree in a particular academic discipline, and then offer some additional instruction in pedagogical technique. Alas, hardly any teacher colleges follow this pattern. Instead, most offer four years of meandering theory and technique, with little depth in any one subject.

Along with subject expertise, the other factor that studies clearly correlate with teacher effectiveness is intelligence. Instructors' literacy levels and verbal abilities, for instance, have been shown to be associated with higher levels of student achievement. You're thinking: "Aha! It's better for teachers to be smart...tell me something I don't already know." But the unfortunate reality is that the typical K-12 teacher produced over the last generation has not even been intellectually average among college graduates.

A host of studies have shown that individuals entering teaching during the 1970s, '80s, '90s, and beyond tended to have lower test scores, lesser academic skills, and poorer GPAs than students who went into other careers. For instance, Vance and Schlechty reported in 1982 that college graduates with low SAT scores were more likely than those with high SATs to enter and remain in the teaching force. Ballou (1996) found that the less selective the college, the more likely that its students entered teaching. McKinsey & Co. discovered that 47 percent of recent entries into teaching had college-entrance test scores in the bottom third of their class. Only 23 percent of new teachers scored in the top third, according to this 2010 report. The authors noted that in countries with top-performing educational systems, like South Korea, Finland, and Singapore, 100 percent of all teachers are drawn from the top third of their academic cohort.

During the latest decade, the rising demand from charter schools for smart teachers, and the growth of alternative recruiting networks like Teach For America and TNTP, has drawn a higher quality of candidate into the profession. Dan Goldhaber and Joe Walch compared the SAT scores of new teachers to college graduates going into all other fields. In the winter 2014 issue of *Education Next* they reported that while in 2001 teachers had ranked 3-7 percentile points below classmates, by 2009 they were two to three points above non-teachers. Still not academic stars, but trending in the right direction.

There is good research showing that the individuals hired to teach in charter schools are more likely to be graduates of selective colleges than teachers in conventional schools. A 2004 paper from the Education Policy Center at Michigan State University compared a weighted mix of 20,000 teachers at conventional and charter schools, and found that the charter teachers were significantly more likely to have graduated from a college that *Barron's Profiles of American Colleges* placed in one of their three most selective categories, and less likely to come out of a

> It is relatively straightforward to track what students know when they start with an instructor and what they know at the end of the year, and then reward or remediate teachers based on the actual record of improvement or stagnation among their students.

non-selective or less-selective college. A 2009 paper by Steven Wilson zeroed in on charter schools that get good results from low-income children and found that 77-83 percent of their teachers came from one of *Barron's* three top categories. (And about two thirds of those came out of a college in the very highest category.) Among teachers in conventional schools, only 19-25 percent graduated from colleges rated in those same selective categories.

Teachers who make their pupils better
The good news is that once they are in classrooms, we don't have to guess who the good teachers are. We can look at the performance of their students. By tracking how much progress pupils make during a year in a given teacher's classroom (as measured in average results

on standardized tests), we get a very concrete indication of whether this is a teacher capable of making a positive difference in the lives of children. Paper qualifications don't matter; the classroom record does.

Over time, every teacher builds up a set of student performance outcomes. These are relatively easy for economists to study. And when economists do so (making proper adjustments for the demographic traits of students, to make certain that apples are being compared to apples), they find that the difference between spending a year with a good teacher versus a bad teacher can easily exceed a full grade of annual growth. For instance, a bad teacher might move his typical students only a half year ahead in knowledge during the same school year when a good teacher moved similar students ahead by a year-and-a-half worth of learning.

It's not easy, but it has been shown that good teachers can get good results even in bad schools, even with children with checkered previous records, with pupils of all races and economic classes. And the effects of good, or bad, teaching are cumulative. Get several teachers of one sort or the other in a row, and the overall educational effect will be pronounced.

An important recent study by economists Raj Chetty, John Friedman, and Jonah Rockoff tracked almost 12,000 pupils for more than 20 years and found that the effects of good teachers and poor teachers could be traced directly to later adult outcomes like going to college, becoming a single parent, saving for retirement, and job earnings. The economists calculated that replacing a poor teacher with a teacher who is merely average would raise the lifetime earnings of the classroom of children who spent one year studying under them by a total of $266,000.

"If you leave a low value-added teacher in your school for ten years, rather than replacing him with an average teacher, you are hypothetically talking about $2.5 million in lost income," summarized professor John Friedman of Harvard. "The message," he underlined, "is to fire people sooner rather than later."

Prominent education researcher Eric Hanushek of Stanford has long argued that the bottom 5 to 10 percent of teachers, judged by the annual scores of their students, should be let go every year. Legendary CEO Jack Welch did this with General Electric's workforce, building it into the most productive of any corporation in America. In Chapter 3, we described Neerav Kingsland's proposal for improving educational quality by shutting down the weakest 5 percent of schools every year (as measured in annual performance scores), and how this would gradually cumulate into a dramatic increase in overall school effectiveness. Removing the worst performing 5 percent of teachers in a system every year would be a more selective way of doing the same thing. The big winners would be children—especially the minority and low-income youngsters who, research shows, are especially helped by higher teacher quality.

There is a whole movement today on behalf of what is called "value-added" teaching. It urges school administrators to use the most straightforward and significant measure available to us—annual improvements in student performance—as a major factor in deciding which teachers should be hired, promoted, paid better, and fired. Since students sometimes enter the classroom far behind where they should be, outright student performance can be an unfair measure; but how far the student moves ahead during the year from wherever he started is an excellent way to identify an effective teacher. School districts in Washington, D.C., Houston, and other places have already begun using value-added metrics to raise their level of teaching and overall school quality.

The first major academic assessment of D.C.'s new system of teacher evaluation, done by James Wyckoff of the University of Virginia and Thomas Dee of Stanford, was released late in 2013. It showed that a rigorous value-added approach to grading teachers has clear positive effects in both retaining good teachers and pushing out persistently ineffective ones. Half of a teacher's evaluation score in D.C. now comes from how much her students improved their standardized test scores after a year in her classroom. Other measures of increased student achievement, plus five classroom observations by principals and master teachers, are also used to grade teachers.

Instructors in D.C. with a value-added score that shows them to be "highly effective" get a cash bonus of up to $27,000. Two "highly effective" ratings in a row lead to a salary raise of as much as $25,000. Getting repeated "highly effective" scores yields the equivalent of about a five-year jump on the standard teacher salary scale. As you might expect, this resulted in higher rates of retention by the district of excellent teachers.

On the other hand, Washington teachers who get reviewed as "ineffective" are subject to dismissal, as are those rated "minimally effective" for two straight years, and those scoring for three years in a row at the middling level of "developing." During the first couple years of the new assessment system, 500 teachers with poor ratings for effectiveness were let go from the D.C. Public Schools.

Washington's assessment system offers coaching and other help for poor performers to improve their classroom practice. Because the coaches have the detailed performance reviews to work from, they can personalize the professional help needed by each teacher, rather than offering general training like typical teacher-development seminars. The study found evidence that teachers at the margins were incentivized to use this professional assistance—those with one low rating sought help to avoid a second, and those near the top of the middle rating made efforts to become "highly effective."

Value-added teacher assessment is one of the more promising strands of education reform today. Conventional schools, however, with their union contracts and other regulatory constraints, sometimes find it hard to put into effect, despite prompting by everyone from free-market economists to President Obama's Department of Education. The fact is, D.C.'s program was pushed through only after a group of major philanthropists, including the Walton, Robertson, Arnold, and Broad foundations, put up $60 million of financial sweetener for teachers—and even still the program's creator, Michelle Rhee, was eventually pushed out of her public office after long teacher-union opposition.

Charter schools, with their comparative lack of political and regulatory restraints, have more opportunity to act on today's powerful new understanding of teacher effectiveness. If they energetically apply value-added measurement to teaching, they will lead the nation in raising the overall quality of school instruction. Philanthropic support could greatly speed that.

The Gates Foundation has been a prominent supporter of serious teacher assessment. They are working on many levels to bring the same kinds of annual measurements, rewards, and accountability to teaching that exist in other professions. In 2009, Gates unveiled a $335 million venture to build teacher effectiveness, including $45 million of spending intended to pioneer and then spread rigorous new systems of teacher evaluation.

Expanding the supply of excellent teachers

Many schools today, including charters, do not have as many truly impressive teachers and teacher candidates as they need or would like. "The charter sector has spent most of its resources frantically expanding the number of 'no excuses' charter schools that depend on highly talented people," explains Rick Hess, director of education policy studies at the American Enterprise Institute. "Staffing all these new schools, including thousands of additional ones to come over the next decade, while also replacing teachers who retire, fail, or burn out, will be a strain in the future. It will only become manageable if we find innovative new ways to effectively train top teachers, reduce unnecessary burdens on them, and incentivize them to stay with education as a career."

Gretchen Crosby Sims of the Chicago-based Joyce Foundation notes that while "charter schools face disadvantages in areas like lacking access to funding for buildings, and getting lower per-pupil reimbursements from states, they also have great advantages. One of the biggest ones is greater flexibility in deploying their teachers. As a result, we as funders should increasingly focus on encouraging strong teachers to flow into the charter sector."

Philanthropy has been crucial in supporting Teach For America, TNTP, and other groups that are bringing impressive new teachers into charter schools.

Lots of organizations have begun efforts to create more good teachers to staff charter schools. Teach For America, which recruits top college graduates and young professionals to teach for at least two years in schools serving needy populations, has moved aggressively into the charter realm in the past several years. Many big urban school districts are losing students and laying off teachers, making it harder for TFA to place its corps members in conventional schools. But the blossoming of charter schools has more than picked up the slack. In Chicago during the 2013-2014 school year, 59 percent of TFA teachers were working in charter schools. In Philadelphia, an even larger fraction work in charters—only 21 out of 257 corps members taught in conventional public schools in that city in 2013. Nationwide, about two thirds of all TFA teachers work in conventional district schools, but the fastest growing niche for TFAers is charter schools.

TFA is of course a product of enlightened philanthropy. Don and Doris Fisher were crucial funders of the initial nationwide expansion of the organization. The Eli and Edythe Broad Foundation, the Laura and John Arnold Foundation, the Robertson Foundation, and Steve and Sue Mandel each provided $25 million in 2011 to create a $100 million long-term endowment for the organization. Even as TFA has grown explosively, two thirds of its annual funding continues to be donated by individuals, foundations, or corporations. Philanthropy has been particularly crucial in supporting TFA's powerful new presence in charter schools, and the group's ability to further increase the number of corps members operating in charters will depend upon continued and expanded donor support.

TNTP, founded in 1997 as the New Teacher Project, is also paying much more attention to charter schools in search of opportunities to jumpstart teacher quality. Originally, TNTP served only conventional district schools. Basing its experts in district offices, the organization would help these large urban bureaucracies recruit, train, and hire new teachers, particularly in hard-to-fill specialties like special-ed and math. The group still does this, through its TNTP Academy, which has so far recommended to districts nearly 3,000 teacher hires. Non-traditional but talented teaching candidates are located, trained, and certified by the Academy, and they have proven to be substantially more effective, on average, than other teachers in the district—performing at a level high enough to more than make up for the average lag in academics found among children from low-income families.

Since 2000, TNTP has also operated a separate Teaching Fellows program. This program looks for accomplished professionals and recent college graduates who weren't schooled or certified as educators but have subject knowledge and talents to help high-need students. The program is extremely selective—only 8 percent of all applicants make it to the classroom. Here again, recruits are particularly steered into the hardest-to-fill jobs: about 40 percent of TNTP Teaching Fellows go into special education, 15 percent teach science, 12 percent teach math, and 10 percent work in bilingual education. More than 32,000 unusually effective teachers have come out of the program since its creation, and increasing numbers of these are being channeled into charter schools.

TNTP charges schools a fee for providing them with a highly qualified teacher. The remaining third of the group's revenue comes from philanthropists.

There are other entities working to raise the caliber of classroom leader available to charter, district, and parochial schools. ACE—the Alliance for Catholic Education—is a kind of TFA that prepares top college graduates to work in Catholic schools, thanks to the support of many donors.

EdFuel is a nonprofit, hatched with support from the Walton Family Foundation and others, which seeks to promote education as a multifaceted field into which professionals of all sorts can enter. EdFuel matches lawyers, IT specialists, human resource managers, advocacy experts, and others to opportunities in education, including at charter schools.

Donors eager to help raise teacher quality at charter schools should be aware of the National Center on Teacher Quality, one of the nation's leading voices on educator effectiveness. The center produces valuable research and advocacy that aims to pull the entire teaching profession up to higher levels of output. Their new 2013 handbook *Teacher Prep Review*, for instance, evaluates 1,100 different colleges on how well they prepare their graduates to become K-12 instructors.

Charter schools themselves have also taken direct action to upgrade the quality of teachers available to their students. For instance, the 38 charter schools in the Harmony network in Texas (which places a special emphasis on mathematics, science, and computer science) have a creative program that brings them strong math and science instructors. With support from the Cosmos Foundation, Harmony finds teachers with deep content knowledge in math and science who are living overseas but interested in working in the U.S. The school helps them secure legal working papers, and brings them to Texas to instruct students.

New ways of training teachers

Several charter school networks have started their own graduate schools of education to prepare new teachers to work in charter schools. These graduate schools meet an important need of charter networks that is rarely filled by conventional teacher prep programs: rigorous training that focuses entirely on demonstrable improvements in student academic performance. Most of these new training regimens require candidates to work in local charter schools while earning their degrees, and they focus relentlessly on practical techniques that have been show to get classroom results.

One of the most exciting of these new teacher prep programs is the Relay Graduate School of Education, the brainchild of three of the most accomplished creators of charter schools in the nation. Dave Levin, Norman Atkins, and Dacia Toll (leaders of the KIPP, Uncommon Schools, and Achievement First charter school networks, respectively) were constantly short on great teachers. What if they built from scratch a dramatically different teacher college capable of turning smart, persistent young people into master educators?

Within months of their first 2005 discussion, Levin, Atkins, and Toll began to pull together a business plan. Then hedge-fund founder Larry Robbins, who was already a big supporter of charter schools, pledged $10 million to get the grad school off the ground. Next, the Robin Hood Foundation, the high-octane New York City philanthropy founded by financier Paul Tudor Jones, raised an additional $20 million for the new college in one night in 2007. Relay opened its doors in 2008, originally housed at Hunter College, where the dean of the education school was an enthusiastic supporter.

The two-year course of study combines best practices unearthed by actual teachers practicing their craft at Uncommon Schools, KIPP, Achievement First, and other top charters. There are three distinctive qualities to the Relay curriculum: 1) Its strong preference for practical techniques proven to work with needy children, rather than educational theory. 2) Use of new technology: More than 40 percent of coursework is delivered online, and intensive video recording is done of each enrollee's classroom instruction, for later study and dissection. 3) A demand for measurable results: Fully half of the program's graduation credits are tied to measured student outcomes, and to receive a master's degree from Relay, you must demonstrate that your pupils made at least a full year's worth of academic growth in one year of school time.

Relay was the first new graduate school of education to be founded in New York City in 80 years. As of 2013 it had already been expanded to two other locales, and was training about 850 teachers in New York, New Orleans, and Newark, New Jersey. Its training is in demand from teachers for conventional schools as well as charters. There are plans to open campuses in Houston and Chicago in 2014 and to establish sites in many other regions after that.

"We hope that in a decade we are able to serve thousands of teachers in cities across the country," says Atkins. "If we want to turn on the next generation of K-12 students, it's essential that we magnetize the most talented and promising college graduates to the teaching profession, and offer them an on-ramp and training that will bring out their very best over the long haul."

Charter schools have already birthed their own teacher colleges in other locations as well. The southern California charter school network High Tech High has opened its own state-approved graduate school of education in San Diego, California. "California needs an estimated 3,300 new math and science teachers each year," points out Larry Rosenstock, founder and CEO of

High Tech High. "Yet the massive University of California system credentials only 210 new math and science teachers per year."

Since the teacher school began in 2007, it has not only ensured a steady flow into High Tech High of new talent that is specifically trained for its classrooms, but also supplied educators to other area charter and conventional schools. The program offers a master's degree in education with two concentrations: school leadership, for individuals who wish to found or run an innovative school, and teacher leadership, for experienced instructors who want to deepen their practice.

Tuition is subsidized and students learn and work alongside teachers and administrators in the High Tech High network of schools. To make

> California needs an estimated 3,300 new math and science teachers each year. Yet the massive University of California system credentials only 210 per year.

access easy, both this graduate school and Relay offer about half of their instruction on line, the rest on site. Philanthropic support for this innovation has been provided by the Amar Foundation, the Ronald Simon Family Foundation, and the James Irvine Foundation.

Match Charter Schools, a network of superb charters in Boston, has created a similar program. Its Sposato Graduate School of Education is a new, independent, state-approved teacher college. Enrollment is extraordinarily competitive—about 100 candidates are enrolled each year out of the 1,500 who get an interview.

The promising "residents" who are selected train as tutors in a Match charter school Monday through Thursday. They work with the same small group of six to seven students for a year, often building one-on-one relationships with the students while providing the support they need to become college ready. On Fridays and Saturdays, the residents attend graduate-school classes and participate in intensive simulations and student teaching.

In their first year of this graduate program, enrollees will each go through about 500 lifelike teaching simulations, which include touches like students walking out and misbehaving at times. Candidates learn techniques for increasing rigor and keeping students engaged. Match CEO Stig Leschly, who founded Match with a large donation of his own money after building Exchange.com and then selling it to Amazon for $200 million, explains that "they practice moves, they scrimmage, then they get their own classrooms."

After a full year of this intensive schedule, residents receive a Massachusetts teachers' license and are offered full-time teaching positions in charter schools in Boston and elsewhere throughout the country. At the end of their first full year of teaching, residents are evaluated and, if found to be performing well, awarded a Master's in Effective Teaching.

Some charters are working on ways of extending the reach of good teachers. On the campuses of Rocketship Education, students spend a portion of their day mastering basic skills via computer instruction. The software frees teachers from repetitive tasks, so they can spend more time filling individual learning gaps and teaching higher-order thinking skills to students in small groups. Teachers also have time to collaborate more, plan more, and participate in more professional development opportunities. Students reap the biggest benefit: Rocketship's model helped it become the leading public school system for low-income students in California in 2012, as measured by scores on the California Academic Performance Index.

So-called blended learning models like Rocketship's, mixing human and computer instruction, are growing fast. (*Blended Learning: A Wise Giver's Guide to Supporting Tech-assisted Teaching*, published in 2013 by The Philanthropy Roundtable, is the definitive guide on this subject.) In addition to freeing teachers from drudge work, giving them much more information on each student's individual progress (thanks to software which regularly spits out individual achievement reports), and opening opportunities for teachers to redesign and customize their classrooms in entrepreneurial ways, blended learning offers one other important advantage in an era where masterful teachers are the scarcest resource: The school doesn't need as many teachers per enrolled student.

By relying on computer instruction and roving teacher's aides to supply much basic instruction and practice, and reserving teachers for complex instruction, the typical Rocketship school requires six fewer teachers per school. That allows better pay per teacher, and provides operational savings which are used to create new schools. It also softens the problem of truly gifted teachers being in short supply. If an administrator only needs to find two or three good new instructors every year instead of four or five, that is a much more manageable hire.

Rocketship has also been lauded for its system of training and developing teachers. It uses frequent feedback from master instructors, including live coaching in the classroom via ear pieces. Once they are developed, the school tries to hang onto its good teachers by promoting all of their future school leaders from their own teacher ranks, rather than recruiting externally.

Developing and hanging onto top talent is an urgent need across U.S. K-12 education. Nationwide, close to 50 percent of all of our teachers leave the profession within five years, with rates being highest in schools full of low-income pupils (which most charter schools are). Research indicates that working conditions are the primary driver in a teacher's decision to leave a school or the profession, and the demanding work conditions in inner-city schools can wear down even the most committed people.

Education scholar Rick Hess argues that finding ways to reduce the need for super-teachers in the future will be an essential part of sustaining the charter school revolution. Pushing for better-than-typical results can be stressful, burning out instructors after a number of years. Unionization (which Hess believes would make many charters indistinguishable from conventional schools in terms of results achieved) becomes a risk. And as the charter sector grows larger, principals have to dig ever deeper in the personnel barrel.

Charters need to use their extraordinary autonomy to develop models for delivering great education without over-reliance on heroic educators, who will always be in limited supply. There are systems that show great promise. Match schools, for instance, delegate much basic instruction to talented tutors who flow through classrooms in groups on one- or two-year contracts. (Many of these are recent college grads testing the waters in education before attending graduate school.) The tutors liberate teachers and let them focus on higher-order instruction that is less likely to lead to burnout. Another model that lessens the demand for saint-level teaching effort is blended learning. Schools like Carpe Diem and Rocketship use computerized instruction to free up teachers and reduce stress, just as Match's system does with tutors.

Elevating principals and new school founders

In addition to excellent teachers, charter schools must have strong, adept administrators. Savvy principals, skilled business managers, and entrepreneurial school executives are needed to handle the operational independence that the charter system pushes down to the individual school level. Without strong leaders, charters will only be free to flounder.

Very good, philanthropically supported programs now exist to help address the shortage of talented school leaders of this sort. Charter school incubators in many regions now offer training and support to individuals who are preparing to open new schools. There are also national programs to develop educational leaders—like the Building Excellent Schools Fellowship supported by dozens of foundation and individual donors. Chapter 2 reviewed some of these incubators in detail.

To meet the strong interest in finding and cultivating charter school leaders from minority backgrounds, the Charter School Growth Fund created Partners for Developing Futures, a venture fund that invests in high-potential charter schools founded or overseen by a minority leader, and serving minority and low-income students. "Partners serves the important dual mission of helping to promote minority leadership while creating additional quality public education options for underserved stu-

Without strong leaders, charters will only be free to flounder.

dents," says Howard Fuller, board chairman for the Black Alliance for Educational Options, and a member of Partners' advisory board. "We see a great need for more support for leaders of color who show potential in the charter sector."

Other leadership programs focus on a particular place, or train leaders for a specific chain of charter schools. The Mind Trust, whose work in Indianapolis as a charter school incubator was discussed in Chapter 2, also has programs to develop school leaders. Its Education Entrepreneur Fellowship brings ambitious reformers to its home city for two years of full-time paid training in the factors to go into high-quality schooling. Their graduates get seed funding and are connected to various community partnerships that can help them launch new schools.

The Indianapolis-based Richard M. Fairbanks Foundation has provided the Mind Trust with $4.5 million in funding for this purpose. What makes the investment so unique is that Fairbanks is not generally an education funder, but rather focuses on health, sustainable employment, and the economic vitality of the foundation's home city. However, they now see flourishing charter schools as an important way to boost prosperity and quality of life in Indianapolis.

As the top-performing networks of charter schools have grown, several have addressed the field's talent shortages by developing their own internal pipelines for teachers and leaders. The KIPP Fisher Fellowship, for example, provides training to educators that will equip them for the demanding job of operating a school within the KIPP network. KIPP absorbs the roughly $200,000 cost of forming each Fisher Fellow (which includes recruitment, selection, instruction, and salary). With major support from the Doris & Donald Fisher Fund, the Broad Foundation, and other donors, the year-long training program includes a residency period in a high-flying KIPP school, as well as intensive coursework at New York University's Steinhardt School of Culture, Education, and Human Development. KIPP accepts fewer than 7 percent of applicants to participate in this selective and demanding fellowship—and all recipients already have several years of teaching experience, including demonstrated results among low-income students. KIPP has trained 125 of its principals in this way, men and women who have gone on to lead new KIPP schools in 20 states and the District of Columbia.

Other charter school leadership programs are based out of universities. In 2013, the Relay Graduate School of Education added a track for training school executives. It retains the school's practical emphases on effective teaching, and shows principals how they can offer instructional leadership in their schools, but then adds the many management skills a school administrator needs. In its first season, 150 principals from around the country took part in Relay's yearlong program.

The Rice Education Entrepreneurship Program has offered principal training at Rice University's Jesse Jones Graduate School of Management since 2008. What's distinctive about the REEP model is that it occurs entirely within a business school. The two-year, MBA-granting program offers intensive immersion in educational entrepreneurship, and turns out principals ready to plan, build, and manage impressive schools. REEP is heavily subsidized by Houston-area philanthropies, so students only have to pay a small portion of the costs, and they can have their loans forgiven if they work in an area school after graduation.

A program similar to REEP was launched in Chicago the same year. The Ryan Fellowship, a joint venture of Northwestern University's Kellogg School of Management and the Accelerate Institute, brings aspiring school leaders to a top business school. They learn the skills and habits of effective educational entrepreneurship, thanks to donor support.

The Accelerate Institute is a nonprofit that offers an array of educational programs. In addition to the Ryan Fellowship, it operates the Inner City Teaching Corps, which brings recent college graduates and mid-career professionals to Chicago's urban classrooms for two years of service as a teacher. The institute also sponsors the Alain Locke Charter School, recognized by the U.S. Department of Education for its effectiveness at closing achievement gaps.

The funder and visionary behind the Accelerate Institute is Patrick Ryan—a former Chicago teacher and narcotics cop who went on to create a successful software company known as Incisent Technologies. Through his several training and operating philanthropies, he has been a spark plug behind the growth of charter schools in the Chicago area. Donors aiming to cultivate charter leaders in their home towns might learn from Accelerate's ventures.

Cultivating leadership at the top

As the charter school sector has mushroomed in size and matured in sophistication, funders have increasingly realized the importance of grooming new and talented leaders for the very top tiers of educational management as well. "We need to change public education from a tired, government monopoly to a high-performing public enterprise," urges Eli Broad, one of the country's top education donors. "To do that you need better people in management and governance who can create the conditions that allow students and teachers to succeed."

With that goal in mind, Broad's foundation created the Broad Residency in Urban Education. It takes executives who have proven themselves professionally, usually in sectors other than education, and places them in two-year, full-time, paid positions within urban school systems, where they solve specific problems while gaining wide educational experience. Most Broad Residents have business, public policy, or law degrees, which they use to improve management practices in urban education. During their residency, participants receive intensive professional development, and after their stints are over, nine out of ten graduates choose to remain in education. There are Broad Residents today in many of the most important charter school networks, in the headquarters of 50 urban school systems, and in state and metropolitan departments of education.

The Broad Foundation also joined with the Michael & Susan Dell Foundation and other donors to create Education Pioneers. This group recruits, carefully screens, and then supports graduate students in education but also fields like finance, human resources, marketing, law, or business strategy, and aims them toward careers in educational management. Education Pioneers awardees serve fellowships at charter or district schools or other educational organizations solving specific operational issues. Afterward, many remain in education on either a full-time or part-time basis. Like the Broad Residency, the generous philanthropic funding behind Education Pioneers allows it to offer competitive stipends and high-level supervision from experienced and successful leaders. Charter networks like Green Dot Public Schools, Victory Schools, Achievement First, Aspire Public Schools, KIPP, and Uncommon Schools have collaborated on projects with Education Pioneers, often leading to job offers.

Another program that relies on philanthropic funding to cultivate and train top school leaders is New Schools for New Orleans. NSNO is a nonprofit set up to transform public education in New Orleans, where more than eight out of ten students now attend charter schools. The organization has created its own in-house training program for educators interested in expanding successful single campuses into other locations. These leaders complete a specialized curriculum and receive direct one-on-one consulting on management and operational skills from local CEOs. The program brings out both a cooperative spirit that invites frank discussion of challenges and a competitive drive that inspires each member to try to produce the best performance in the city.

For more on the important topic of improving the quality of school teachers and leaders, you should consult the Roundtable's book dedicated entirely to that topic—*Excellent Educators: A Wise Giver's Guide on Cultivating Great Teachers and Principals*, published in April 2014.

Board development

A final leadership role that is important to school success, yet not especially well supported by the current helping infrastructure that charter school leaders look to for practical assistance, is development of a school's board. Every charter school needs a board, and they can make or break the facility—since charters operate outside of district bureaucracies, wise oversight is crucial. Yet, while a goodly number of organizations exist today to help charters recruit and train teachers, principals, and other staff, there are few that offer the specialized knowledge needed to lock in strong school-board members. It may be time for charter school backers to support a sustained effort that will aid school founders in finding and cultivating first-rate leaders for their boards.

Frequently, boards end up dominated by one particular group—educators in some cases, business leaders in others, often initial founders or donors. But charter schools require a broad array of skills to operate successfully throughout a period of years, and pulling a broader pool of talent and experience onto a board can help solve many problems. Another problem today is that members serving on a charter-school board don't always fully appreciate the breadth of their responsibilities. To address this, some schools and support organizations have developed written guides for board members. One group of funders has gone even further, creating training seminars for all board candidates. At Brighter Choice Charter Schools in Albany, New York, every incoming board member attends a hands-on seminar that prepares him or her for service.

An alternative to funding board improvements at individual schools is to fund an intermediary organization specializing in board development that will work at many different schools. Charter Board Partners and the High Bar are two entities that specialize in this work. Charter Board Partners will help recruit boards by carefully vetting candidates with a range of talents, matching them to appropriate charter schools, and then providing ongoing training and networking opportunities. Initially focused on Washington, D.C., Charter Board Partners is now preparing to expand nationally. The High Bar, based in the Boston area, already has a national clientele. They have partnered with more than 200 charter schools in 20 states, analyzing the strengths and weaknesses of various boards, assigning targeted board training, and offering helpful tools and management systems.

Encouraging Public Policies that Help Charters Flourish

If charter schools are to truly thrive, the philanthropic investments discussed in this book will not be enough. States will also need to adopt charter-friendly public policies. We have a ways to go in this area.

There are still eight states—Kentucky, Nebraska, Vermont, West Virginia, North Dakota, South Dakota, Montana, and Alabama—that flatly disallow chartering. There are six other states that have only trivial numbers of charter schools (in the single digits). States like Maryland, Virginia, Iowa, Kansas, Mississippi, and Wyoming burden charters with suffocating regulations (applications often require hundreds and hundreds of pages of paperwork), constrict the number of schools or authorizers, or seriously underfund charters in comparison to conventional schools.

In Virginia, for instance, only local school boards are allowed to authorize charters, and any schools these authorities decide to allow to operate must operate under that district's personnel policies and union agreement—effectively outlawing the flexible staffing that is central to charter success. Virginia funding for charter schools is parsimonious and indeed nonexistent in many crucial categories. And charters must be reapplied for every few years in Virginia, where the process is laborious.

The Center for Education Reform rates charter school laws every year. In their latest report card, only 13 states earned an A or B for the quality of their charter law. And within states there are often regions and cities where the law is applied unevenly, limiting local access to charters.

Even in average-to-better states, the public financing for charter schools is routinely lower than what is paid to district schools. Nationwide, the funding offered to charter schools for each child enrolled averages only 80 percent of what it is for conventional schools. In urban districts, per-child funding for charters is just 72 percent of what other public schools get. Only if charter school supporters cry foul and push for more equitable formulas will these per-child allotments to the millions of youngsters in charter schools be made fairer.

There are restrictions on a foundation's ability to involve itself in public advocacy. (See the chart "What's Allowed...?" later in this chapter, and consult an experienced attorney for particulars.) Nonetheless, there remain many ways in which funders can help make the case to both policymakers and the general populace on behalf of more charter-friendly public policies. Savvy funders have become very active on this front over just the last few years, because they found they had to.

"Our goal has always been to create more high-quality options for more low-income children. But we learned that many times that depends on the regulatory and legislative environment surrounding charter schools," says Jim Blew, director of K-12 education reform at the

Walton Family Foundation. So new tactics were tried. "Investments in the policy arena can be very powerful means toward creating healthy and flourishing schools."

"The best amount to give to policy work will vary from state to state, and city to city," explains Neerav Kingsland of New Schools for New Orleans. "First, a donor should determine what her goals are for charter growth. Then she should examine what the central requirements are for that to occur: Fixing policy obstructions? Developing school leaders? Finding teacher talent? Cultivating community support? Take a look at your specific circumstances and divvy funds accordingly."

Dipping into a big tool bag

As we'll discuss throughout this chapter, changing policy often demands a range of interventions, from research to public relations to direct lobbying. An essential starting point for philanthropists is to support the professional organizations and affinity groups that have sprung up across the country to explain and promote the interests of charter schools.

> Keep the regulatory arm of the government at bay so charter schools can do what they do best: spend money differently, use technology differently, reconfigure how students spend time learning.

Donors can also be very helpful in paying for basic problem analysis. A donor might compile lists of unfriendly laws and regulations so they can be revised. Another could calculate and spell out the precise ways that the financing formulas discriminate against charters. This kind of public-interest research is prime territory for enlightened philanthropic support.

Lightening the bureaucratic load on charters can be a vital public service. "If we're tasking these schools with succeeding in the same neighborhoods and with the same populations where traditional schools have failed, they have to be allowed to innovate. That means protecting them from getting burdened with regulation," argues former Arnold Foundation vice president Caprice Young. Nina Rees of the National Alliance for Public Charter Schools agrees. "Keep the regulatory arm of the government at bay so charter schools can do what they do best—spend money differently, use technology differently, reconfigure how students spend time learning."

Leading donor Katherine Bradley urges civic leaders: "Don't just act like a regulator to all these incredible operators who want to come do this work. Make it easy for them. They need the freedom to tell their best leaders 'You can change your hours. You can change your curriculum. You don't need to follow the pattern here.' They need to be able to give each of their campuses more autonomy. Those things help performance. It may be messy, but they need to be able to do that in order to succeed."

Another way funders can be helpful is to aid schools, and the sector as a whole, in creating savvy public-relations strategies. "This is a huge opportunity, and there is a very big need for donors to help with this," says Christopher Nelson, whose Doris & Donald Fisher Fund incubated KIPP and other exemplary charter schools. "We have to figure out how to brand and message these schools more positively" in the face of attacks from opponents, suggests Nelson. The Fisher Fund is a leader here, having created a specific division that provides public-relations consulting to all of the schools they give grants to.

There is a dedicated Fisher employee who handles all of KIPP's communications. Some of the principles that he has followed in the past:

- as soon as a school has results, share them via report cards
- be candid when schools don't meet standards
- focus on relationships with parents; it's crucial that families like the school
- built relationships with pastors, business leaders, others in the community
- encourage schools to have an open-door policy with reporters; get them into classrooms

The kind of direct service that Fisher offers its grantees could be copied by other funders if they have the expertise. Or money could be earmarked so schools can hire freelance assistance with communications. Nelson suggests that, "donors can fund people like Gary Larson to help with crisis management or framing longer-term messaging and media relationships. Our charter school movement in California would not be where it is today without his sound advice. He and others like him are necessary. Certain national nonprofits are also figuring out how to be helpful in this area—like StudentsFirst, and the National Alliance for Public Charter Schools."

In general, working directly with local schools and families will be the optimal way to discover what arguments most need to be voiced in a particular region. There are also some broad narratives and facts that could be laid before the public to improve understanding of charters. Few schools have any incentive to spend time or money on that type of long-term image building, though. Foundations could render a public service by taking on some of this meta-storytelling.

An example would be the campaign created by the Laura and John Arnold Foundation to publicize the positive results that have accumulated in New Orleans since Hurricane Katrina destroyed that city's old school structure and sparked a giant shift toward charters. The foundation recently launched an "informational campaign that highlights Louisiana as a national model for transforming public education." In a series of online, print, and radio messages, attention is being drawn to the sharp increases in student competency in New Orleans since its charter explosion took place. Here is a sample ad:

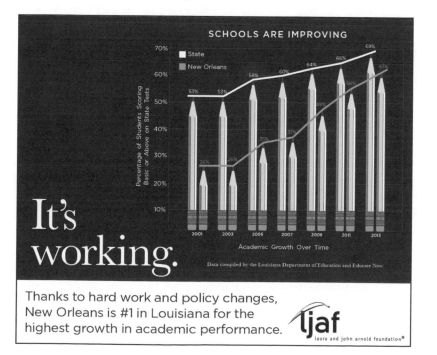

It's worth noting that charitable tax law allows philanthropic organizations to sponsor public educational campaigns, and even educational sessions for policymakers. There is evidence that such sessions on the benefits and proper roles of charter schools can be a low-cost, high-leverage strategy for donors. Victoria Rico of San Antonio's Brackenridge Foundation funded site visits to other places where charters were burgeoning so that key players from her community could observe their potential first hand. The strategy deepened local interest in charters, and by the 2012-13 school year 26 percent of all San Antonio schoolchildren were in charter schools, giving that city the tenth highest market share in the U.S.

Philanthropists hoping to shape the policies under which charter schools operate may sometimes need to act in sectors outside of public opinion and politics. Scholar Rick Hess has suggested a long-term effort at teacher colleges that could be constructive. Philanthropists, he urges, might offer research funds and endowments to schools of education that are willing to support professors who are open-minded about charters (a commodity scarce as dragons' eggs within education schools at the moment). The payoff on such a venture would have to be measured over a decade, but planting and watering inside faculties of education intellectuals who are willing to give charter schools their due could eventually cumulate into important research and policy ideas useful in protecting charters from ideological hostility.

In some locales, donors will want to move beyond research and messaging into more active organizing. Many donors play active roles as "harbormasters" in their cities, connecting schools, families, the public, media, civil rights groups, businesspeople, and local leaders. One of the best ways to safeguard and expand charter schools is to support the building of grassroots coalitions in the communities that benefit from these schools.

Once the ball is rolling, these grassroots efforts often take off on their own and require no further support. Donor Katherine Bradley describes just such a spontaneous success in Washington, D.C.:

> We wanted the vision of charter school success to penetrate so deeply and widely in D.C. that if we got a new less-supportive mayor, he or she would hear from everybody the strategies that work. It's not traditional philanthropy; I don't even know what you'd call it—field-building, maybe—but we spent a good bit

of our time supporting in this area. And now there are hundreds and hundreds of people in D.C. who we don't control at all who go off and start things, and write blogs, and create support groups, all by themselves.

Sometimes litigation is needed to overcome obstacles such as those mentioned in this chapter. Lawsuits are costly, but helpful rulings can echo across hundreds of schools, for decades. In addition to considering particular local battles, there are public-interest legal organizations that methodically defend charter school interests as part of their regular mission. Philanthropists interested in this area might support groups like the Institute for Justice, the Charter School Advocacy Program of the Atlantic Legal Foundation, the Goldwater Institute, and the Landmark Legal Foundation. "Investing in advocates who are fighting in courts of law can be very helpful," notes Nina Rees.

The necessity of politics

Within the past few years, supporters of charter schools have realized that defending and extending these institutions also requires direct participation in politics. Ballot initiatives, accepting appointments on boards and commissions, lobbying, and campaign activity (recruiting candidates, donating money, issue advertising) are sometimes essential. This can be necessary on various local and state levels. Foundations can, by law, only get involved in limited amounts of defensive lobbying, and no politicking whatsoever. But they can support nonprofits dedicated to building grassroots support and engaging in broad advocacy on behalf of charters, including some lobbying. Moreover, donors and their families are free as individuals to make non-tax-deductible payments for direct professional lobbying, gifts to 501(c)(4) organizations that focus on influencing policymakers, donations to 527 groups that inform voters about candidates' positions, or straight contributions to charter-friendly candidates for office. (See chart on page 104 "What's Allowed?" for shorthand descriptions of some of these options.)

"It took me a while to understand that an advocacy and political effort has to go hand-in-glove with the charitable effort," admits education donor Betsy DeVos, who is now also chairwoman of the American Federation for Children, a 501(c)(4) advocacy group. "Ultimately, elected officials make decisions about legislation that can either permit or preclude meaningful educational reform."

"Advocacy does pay off," agrees Jim Blew of the Walton Family Foundation. "We have seen real progress in places like Florida, Louisiana, Indiana, Tennessee, and more recently Georgia and D.C. Reformers would not have succeeded in those places if we sat on the sidelines and didn't get involved in some tough political fights."

"I can tell you from personal experience," Blew continues, "that you get much, much more bang for your charitable buck when you're simultaneously involved in lobbying or elections. It's not twice the impact per dollar. It's an order of magnitude difference per dollar."

"For years when education-reform funders talked about advocacy, they were really talking about communications," says Chester Finn of the Fordham Foundation. "They tended to think that if you made a compelling argument, the reforms would take care of themselves. It took them a while to engage the full spectrum of advocacy efforts."

Finn confesses:

> Like many think-tank types, I'm partial to the somewhat naïve belief that solid data and good analysis will ultimately win. What we came to discover, however, was that the opponents of real reform were not interested in our arguments. They had different incentives and would stoop as low as necessary to thwart any attempt at meaningful change. Reformers eventually realized that they would have to get their hands dirty. Strong-arming policymakers, raising campaign funds, recruiting candidates—it's all politics, with all the messiness and sharp elbows that politics can bring. In that effort, research and analysis are necessary, but not sufficient. We kept bringing flashlights, but you can't fight fire with a flashlight. You have to fight fire with fire.

Victoria Rico of the Brackenridge Foundation will never forget the moment she decided to take the leap and get involved in active advocacy for charter schools. She had just watched the documentary *Waiting for Superman*, which fired her determination to bring high-quality charter schools to her home community of San Antonio.

> The decision to actually go through with the plan is still vivid in my memory. I worried about all of the enemies that I would make; I worried about burning political capital that my family had built up in the community for generations. Ultimately, we

moved forward, and I'm so glad that we did. Yes, we did encounter opponents, but we also attracted many allies from all across the political spectrum. Most importantly, we're now making a huge difference in the lives of disadvantaged children here.

All of these men and women caution that advocacy and politics are not simple tasks. "Make no mistake, advocacy is hard," says Blew. "The teacher unions, the administrators, the school boards—they have very-well-developed infrastructures for both lobbying and political campaigns. The teacher unions have the very best political operation in the country."

Part of this is sheer volume of resources. Keep in mind that in a city like Los Angeles alone, about $23 million is pulled out of teachers' paychecks every year and sent to the union. Much of this is available for politicking.

> We can't just play defense every two years when there's an election. We have to be continually on the offensive as well.

"Don't underestimate the opposition," Blew warns. "They've been at this for years and they're really good at it. To get it right you have to be patient and you have to work over time. If you're not vigilant, the opposition will come back and will overturn your progress in the next cycle."

Neerav Kingsland offers similarly blunt advice: "Know that the unions will oppose charter schools, because they're a threat to the market share of labor. That doesn't mean you have to position yourself as anti-union. Charters can be framed around educator empowerment and giving students options. You just need to be prepared for the arguments."

Where they are unable to block charters altogether, opponents push measures that restrict the ability of the sector to expand or to innovate. Favorite tactics include "freezing" charter school numbers at a low level, often even below existing levels. Or demanding uniform classroom practices that take away the ability of teachers and principals in charters to improvise. Or exactly prescribing the number of minutes schools must devote to particular subjects, again tying the hands of classroom teachers who tend to get better-than-typical results by employing non-typical

What's allowed in policy advocacy?

*Nonprofit organizations that funders can use or create
to promote policy change*

501(c)(3) Private Foundation
(example: Bill & Melinda Gates Foundation)
The crux: Tax exempt. Donations are tax deductible. Contributions and
grants are publicly disclosed. Generally cannot lobby (advocate for specific rules or legislation with elected officials or their staff) except in "self
defense." Can provide funds to charities that lobby with funds from other
sources. Can directly inform public opinion and public policies through
research and communications. Prohibited from engaging in political campaigns. Main advocacy role is to conduct policy research and run pub-
lic-awareness campaigns.

501(c)(3) Public Charity
(example: KIPP)
The crux: Tax exempt. Donations are tax deductible. Contributors can be
anonymous. Can advocate for public policies. Can engage in a limited
amount of lobbying. May engage in nonpartisan election activities like
debates, candidate forums, voter assistance. Prohibited from engaging
in political campaigns. Main advocacy role is to push for public policies it
believes in.

techniques. Opponents even continue to promote the argument, nearly
a quarter century into the charter school revolution, that charters are
unconstitutional. The very favorite argument of charter school opponents is that they are "undemocratic," and suck resources away from
efforts to elevate America's poor and unfortunate.

The best defense against that argument is to let charter school families speak for themselves. Most charter school families are low income—a

501(c)(4) Social Welfare Organization

(example: StudentsFirst)

The crux: Tax exempt. Donations are not tax deductible. Contributors can be anonymous. Can advocate for public policies without limitation. Can lobby without limitation on topics related to its mission. Can participate in political activity, including urging particular votes and depicting candidates in positive or negative ways. Also allowed to engage in active electioneering so long as that is not the "primary purpose of the group," and the electioneering is relevant to the organization's primary purpose. (These same basic rules apply to 501(c)(6) Trade Associations, which often do similar work in the policy arena.)

527 Political Action Committee

(example: National Education Association Fund)

The crux: Tax exempt. Donations are not tax deductible, and they are capped at $5,000 per year. Donors are publicly disclosed. Only minimal lobbying allowed. Can make unlimited contributions to political campaigns, including directly to candidates, subject only to federal reporting and dollar requirements. Main purpose is to directly supply campaign expenses in support of specific candidates, ballot initiatives, or legislation.

527 Independent-expenditure PAC *Also known as a Super PAC*

(example: AFL-CIO Workers' Voices PAC)

The crux: Tax exempt. Donations are not tax deductible, and they are unlimited. Donors are publicly disclosed. Only minimal lobbying allowed. Can make unlimited contributions to political campaigns, subject only to federal reporting and dollar requirements, but these cannot go directly to candidates or be coordinated with candidates. Main purpose is to inform voters of the positions of candidates on public issues, or the merits of ballot initiatives or legislation.

majority of all charter students are eligible for federal school lunch subsidies. Close to seven out of ten charter school students are black, Hispanic, or other minority. Organizing strong and vocal networks of parents and neighborhood allies is extremely helpful in getting regulators and politicians to allow the growth of high-quality charter schools.

Grassroots organizing is also a powerful force for dispelling common myths that perpetuate wariness of charter schools. Philanthropists interviewed for this book agree that one of the charter sector's most pressing weaknesses has been its inability to cement in the public mind a compelling message about what charter schools are and how they can help improve student outcomes. "There is a huge need for donors to help change the perception that charter schools are anti-teacher, or part of a movement to privatize and profit from education," suggests Christopher Nelson of the Fisher Fund. "We need to counter that message and replace it with a more positive one."

"We have great human stories to share," notes Nina Rees. She urges supporters to make sure these stories reach the ears of the wider public, "along with the great data we now have proving that charters can lift children to higher levels of achievement, success, and happiness. On both the national stage and state by state, we need people to hear our message and start demanding more high-quality charter schools in their communities."

Educational consultant Caprice Young agrees that "it's important for us to share positive data, and to organize parents of charter school students— plus parents of students on charter school waiting lists! We also have to be mindful, though, that opposition will not simply fade away when people see high-quality charter schools getting great results. We're demanding a shift in the power structure that is threatening to powerful elements of the status quo. We can't just play defense every two years when there's an election. We have to be continually on the offensive as well."

The grassroots antidote to criticism

Happily, families in low-income communities have demonstrated time and again—in Florida, in New York, in the District of Columbia—that they are quite willing to rise up in large numbers to advocate vigorously for charter schools and other forms of educational choice. Many funders have come to appreciate the need to support and amplify these kinds of popular demonstrations. Savvy donors make it an intrinsic part of their giving to help parents organize and project their voices to policymakers.

Take the Brighter Choice Foundation. It has made Albany, New York, one of the more interesting charter markets in the nation, with 13 charter schools (10 of which receive support from Brighter Choice) in a relatively small city. The foundation has built and protected this market share with aggressive parent organizing. One of their events drew 3,000 students, parents, and community members.

Eva Moskowitz, creator of the Success Charter Network that operates 20 schools in Harlem and other low-income neighborhoods of New

York City, has repeatedly mobilized thousands of parents to attend public hearings to demand much-needed space in public school buildings. As a former city council member and outspoken education committee chair for New York City, Moskowitz has become a political dynamo on behalf of the charter school movement generally.

Families for Excellent Schools trains parents to advocate directly for their local school. It began working with parents who had children in 65 charter schools in New York, New Jersey, and Connecticut, encouraging them to become educational advocates, and training them how to effectively speak and act on their own on behalf of their schools. Director Jeremiah Kittredge previously worked as a public-school teacher and a labor organizer at SEIU, a 2-million-strong union of service workers, so he brings unusual advocacy tools to the table.

The biggest grassroots education rally of recent years was one that donor John Kirtley helped pull together in Tallahassee in 2010. It was the largest political demonstration in Florida's history, gathering 5,600 people in defense of educational alternatives for families. The scene was captured in reporting by *Philanthropy* magazine's Christopher Levenick.

That March morning, thousands of the attendees arrived after overnight bus rides from distant parts of the state. Parents chatted. Clergymen greeted newcomers. Excited schoolchildren clutched signs with hand-lettered slogans like, "Don't Take Away My Dreams," "Education Through Choice," "Put Politics Aside for Me," and "My Future is Priceless." It was a predominantly black and Hispanic crowd, gathered for a single purpose: to convince the Florida legislature to strengthen the state's school choice program.

Marching at the head of the procession, alongside the Reverend H. K. Matthews, an 82-year-old African-American minister who had protested in Selma, Alabama, was John Kirtley. A Tampa venture capitalist who had donated and raised millions to improve schooling for low-income families, he helped organize the march after more than a decade of focused, sustained evolution from a simple funder of charitable efforts into someone who knows how to coordinate his donations with legislative efforts and political giving. Kirtley is a supporter of all forms of school choice, but his story is a case study in effective education-reform advocacy that can guide supporters of charters and public-school choice whether or not they would also advocate for choice systems that give parents access to private and parochial schools.

Kirtley's 501(c)(3) charity Step Up for Students channels money directly to children and families for tuition and other school expenses.

Like all (c)(3) organizations, IRS rules forbid it from asking the public or legislators to support specific legislation. A (c)(3) charity can, however, execute activities like communications, research, and grassroots outreach with policy implications.

Kirtley's 501(c)(3) had long done as much advocacy as the rules allow. It contracted with third-party researchers to test the effectiveness of the schools and programs it supported. To respond to a hostile press, it set up an aggressive communications shop. For president of the 501(c)(3), Kirtley had hired a longtime public-school teacher who was also the former head of the Pinellas County teachers' union.

"It was an interesting situation," Kirtley says. "By statute, all the kids in the program were poor, and I can all but guarantee that their parents vote overwhelmingly Democratic. But their representatives in the

> It took me a while to understand that an advocacy and political effort has to go hand-in-glove with the charitable effort. Elected officials make decisions that can either permit or preclude meaningful educational reform.

legislature consistently voted against this program, and many of them denounced it on the floor. So we needed to educate those parents, so that they would know what their representatives were doing." Step Up for Students hired a grassroots manager who immediately began reaching out to African-American ministers and other community leaders.

Making connections to parents and ministers was one thing, but Kirtley knew he also needed to take his case directly to legislators. A vigorous legislative advocacy campaign would require stepping outside the framework of a 501(c)(3) entity, so Kirtley launched a 501(c)(4) group to handle political issues. This required vigilance to keep strict accounts of their time and resources, so that (c)(3) dollars would not be illegally spent on (c)(4) activities.

With a 501(c)(4) wing, Step Up for Students could now take its case directly to legislators. It was not only a matter of being in Tallahassee and lobbying individual policymakers about pending bills. Now Kirtley and his colleagues could also help their friends and allies reach out. "One of my favorite examples is a radio ad we did in Jacksonville," explains Kirtley. "There was an African-American state senator who was completely opposed to our efforts. Well, we went to his minister and had him tape an ad for us. 'Senator,' the minster's booming voice concluded, *do the right thing.* We aired the ad on all three of Jacksonville's black radio stations." The senator got the message.

Even with the ability to communicate directly with legislators, Kirtley soon realized he needed a third capacity: political engagement. "Early on," he recalls, "I had a very kind African-American state senator take me into his office, close the door, and say, 'John, I know you're right, and I know this is the right thing to do. But I came here to do ten good things. If I do your one good thing, the teachers' union will take me out in the next primary. I will never get to the other nine good things. So I can't do it.'" Kirtley realized that he needed to make it safe for Democratic legislators to vote for the program—and that meant providing the money and muscle to offset the influence of the unions.

The first order of business was creating a 527 Political Action Committee. Under federal law, an independent 527 organization operates to influence the election of candidates to public office, without expressly endorsing a particular candidate or campaign. So long as they register with the IRS, publicly disclose their donors, and file periodic reports, 527s can raise unlimited amounts and use these resources for "electioneering communications."

"Our 527 was able to talk about candidates in a favorable or unfavorable way," explains Kirtley. "But we never used trip-line words like vote for or vote against. We could spend $1 million on a radio ad that said, 'Senator Smith stands for Florida's students—call and thank him!' But we could not and would not pay 33¢ to stamp a single postcard that said, 'Elect Senator Smith!'"

Throughout the course of three election cycles, from 2002 to 2008, Kirtley's independent 527 invested $4.5 million in various legislative races. Most of the money went to primaries. "Florida," notes Kirtley, "is so thoroughly gerrymandered that there are very few contested general election races." Through the 527, Kirtley and his allies became one of the state's largest investors in electioneering communications.

Forming a 527 organization was only one aspect of Kirtley's political efforts. The other involved bundling hard money—personal checks written directly to a candidate's campaign. "Look, campaigns need money to run for office," says Kirtley. "I became a bundler for candidates." He traveled around the country, fundraising from fellow donors who were concerned about schools. He discovered that relatively modest sums could yield real influence. "In Florida," he explains, "an individual can only give $500 per candidate, per election cycle. It's pretty rare to see a candidate in a relatively low-income House district raise more than $30,000 or $40,000 for the primary. So I would go out and try to raise $10,000 to $12,000."

The culmination of this charitable, legislative, and political work came in 2010. On March 23, the day of the march on the state capitol, the Florida Senate cast a historic vote. (The House joined it a day later.) The various school-choice measures that inspired the march passed with strong bipartisan support. "This time, we had Democratic co-sponsors for the bill," smiles Kirtley. "We had a majority of the black caucus, and all but one member of the Hispanic caucus."

"In my experience," concludes Kirtley, "if you want to achieve any real progress in education reform, you cannot just have a (c)(3) capability. You must also have advocacy and political capabilities. If your goal is to change K–12 policy, you're going to have to change K–12 laws. And if legislators refuse to change those laws, then you're going to have to change those legislators."

A treetops strategy can also work

While Kirtley built a mass movement to support new approaches, another way to go is to cultivate and support the emergence of new administrators at the apex of school systems who will try new things. Michael Bloomberg has been one of the pioneers of this strategy. As mayor of New York City, he employed the "new leaders at the top" method to break up ineffective old ways of doing things within his city's massive education bureaucracy.

In 2002, Bloomberg wrestled control of the city's public schools away from the long-dysfunctional New York City Board of Education. The take-charge mayor and the new school chancellor he installed, Joel Klein, then brawled for a full decade to institute ambitious reforms from the summit of their administrative pyramid. They opened scores of promising new charter schools in low-income areas. They closed more than 100 of the system's lowest-performing schools. They rewrote the rules governing teacher tenure (before the new regulations went into effect, 97 percent of eligible teachers received tenure; in 2012, only 57 percent received tenure). They increased the budgetary authority of principals, and raised teacher pay.

Student test scores began a long, slow, steady climb. The Bloomberg method of working from the top down, which has led to disappointment in many cities, showed that it could also succeed, given the right combination of leadership and circumstances. "One way to fix schools is to install leaders who will champion important political and policy change," Bloomberg summarizes. (The next test will be to see if those changes endure now that a mayor with very different priorities has taken over in New York.)

Taking off his mayor's hat and working as a private philanthropist with an estimated net worth of $27 billion, Bloomberg backed efforts similar to his New York City strategy in a few other places. A notable example was Louisiana, which became a crucial laboratory for education reform while rebuilding its post-Katrina school systems. In 2011, Louisiana held important state school board elections.

Bloomberg first helped 36-year-old John White bring his ideas and energy to the state. White was a Teach For America corps member who went on to serve for five years as a top deputy to Joel Klein in New York. In May 2011, White was appointed superintendent of the Louisiana Recovery School District. He hit the ground running, immediately implementing a three-year strategic plan, trimming the central office by one third, and overhauling the failing schools still in the RSD.

Not only Bloomberg but also other education-reform funders nationwide took notice. Working with parents and local reform advocates, they decided to back similar reformers who had declared for the fall elections of the Louisiana Board of Elementary and Secondary Education. Among other duties, that body appoints the Louisiana superintendent of education. Using PAC and 501(c)(4) monies, Bloomberg spent $330,000 to help elect reformist state school-board members. His outside money supplemented local donations of about $500,000 backing the same innovators.

In January 2012, a new board was inaugurated. It had a 9-2 supermajority in favor of school choice and accountability reforms, which included charter schooling. The new board made its first order of business the appointment of John White as superintendent.

As a philanthropist, I "look for places where strong leaders are putting kids first," says Bloomberg. "We look for local leaders who are championing important political and policy changes and making real strides. We look for places where we can help prove what's possible to improve student success on a large scale."

"I'm optimistic that we can succeed," Bloomberg concludes. "Partly because we've seen here in New York City what a difference leaders can make. And partly because I believe the entire country is reaching a tipping point in terms of recognizing the severity of this problem—and demanding action."

Bloomberg's time as mayor has ended, and he is putting even more of his time into philanthropy. If he continues to forcefully back education reformers, Bloomberg could have a large energizing effect on charter school expansion and education innovation generally. "Along with the Gates and Walton families, Bloomberg is an 800-pound gorilla of education reform," says one D.C.-based expert. "Nobody knows exactly what he'll do, but we know it could be really big. He's hiring some of the most impressive people in the field. He is ed reform's $20 billion question mark."

National programs as an alternative to home-grown organizing

Kirtley and Bloomberg are exceptionally involved, enterprising, and well-resourced education philanthropists. But there are plenty of ways for less superhuman donors to mix charitable giving, issue advocacy, lobbying, and political donations in integrated efforts that lend strong positive jolts to the cause of education reform. For philanthropists who don't have the time or money to build their own custom campaigns from scratch like Kirtley and Bloomberg, the simplest method is to fund some of the excellent advocacy now being churned out by groups supported by myriads of donors.

One of the biggest and best organized of these organizations is StudentsFirst, created by Michele Rhee. As in New York City, school powers in Washington, D.C., were stripped from a dysfunctional school board and transferred to the mayor in 2007. After the mayor named Rhee his chancellor of schools, she transformed the horrendous D.C. schools into one of the most exciting reform experiments in the country, with safety, teacher quality, student achievement, and family satisfaction on the rise.

Despite this record, opponents eventually managed to chase the hard-charging Rhee and her boss, mayor Adrian Fenty, out of town. (Rhee's deputy Kaya Henderson picked up her mantle, however, and kept D.C. schools on a brave reform path—such that almost half of all D.C. students now attend charters.) Reeling in the aftermath of her political loss, Rhee asked herself how this had happened.

"I didn't figure in the power of the unions," was her answer. So she went about creating a new national organization aimed at evening the balance of power a bit by making sure the interests of children and their families are represented in future political battles. (This reporting is based on an extensive interview The Philanthropy Roundtable conducted with Michelle Rhee, which is available as a transcript at philanthropyroundtable.org/topic/k_12_education/interview_with_michelle_rhee.)

If education reform was to have any hope of advancing, Rhee and her philanthropic supporters decided, it would need to match the political strength of its opponents. "We settled on a plan to create a national advocacy group that would raise money and build membership with the goal of providing political muscle to leaders who stood for change. We had no name, no staff, no business plan, no location. All we knew was that it was going to be big." There were two concrete goals: a nationwide membership of one million and a budget of $1 billion.

Rhee immediately started reaching out to the country's leading education-reform donors. She called Jim Blew and asked him to request a commitment of $100 million from the Walton family. She went to

> If education reform was to have any hope of advancing, Rhee and her philanthropic supporters decided, it would need to match the political strength of its opponents.

New York to meet with Ted Forstmann, who pledged $50 million. She met with John and Laura Arnold in Houston, Eli and Edythe Broad in Los Angeles, and the Fisher family in San Francisco. With initial funding in place, she looked for a way to draw attention to the new group. In December of 2010, she donned a smart tweed outfit, went on "Oprah," and announced the launch of StudentsFirst.

StudentsFirst is a full-spectrum advocacy effort, with 501(c)(3), 501(c)(4), and 527 PAC capabilities. "I strongly believe that until we can change the laws and policies that are in place," says Rhee, "we're never going to really see a shift in the trajectory of the reform momentum." Much of the effort involves 501(c)(4) issue advocacy, but Rhee notes that "part of it is also electoral work, to be quite frank."

Rhee has seen the phenomenon time and again. "Many politicians will say, behind closed doors, 'Yes, I get your issues. And I agree—I have kids—but I can't do anything about it. The powers that be will not like that. If I go with you, they will run somebody against me, and that would mean I may not be here in the future. And I think the world is a better place if I'm in office.'"

Of all the education-reform advocacy groups, StudentsFirst stands out for the scale of its ambitions. "We are a membership organization with more than two million members across the country," says Rhee. "They are a very active membership, which we've found is crucially important. Not only do you need the dollar resources to back a candidate, but you want boots on the ground, too. If you have people who are willing to knock on doors and man phone banks on behalf of politicians, that is a huge help."

Rhee set a second-year goal of increasing StudentsFirst to two million members. They made it (the lowest level of membership is free and only requires professing support and providing an e-mail address). "For our third year, we are actually changing the focus. We're putting much less emphasis on membership acquisition, because we feel like two million members is a very strong base on which to build."

The new goal is inspiring a committed group of activists. "What we are focused on now is growing the number of what we call our core," says Rhee, "people who not only are opening and reading our e-mails and will take an occasional action here or there, but people who are willing to go out there and mobilize their neighbors to lead the charge. We have a goal of having several hundred of what we call transformation team leaders, and active transformation teams all over the country through our third year."

StudentsFirst doubled its expenditures in each of its first years. Financial support for the group now extends way beyond the initial group of mega-philanthropists who helped Rhee launch. A wide base of small and medium donors is central to the organization's strength.

"Our goal is to achieve a steady state of about $200 million a year," she explains. "A lot of people look at that number and say, 'Well, that's just *astronomical*. What are you going to do with $200 million every year?' Well, let's compare that with other advocacy groups that we're fighting against every day." The two national teacher unions, Rhee points out, have an annual budget of $2.2 billion, and they spend at least $500 million on political activity.

The reform agenda for StudentsFirst is broad and sweeping. At its heart, it boils down to three key areas: elevating the teaching profession, empowering parents, and spending taxpayer dollars wisely. "There are 37 specific policies for which we advocate within those three areas," says Rhee. "Whether it's a fight to lift the charter cap in New York or the constitutional amendment in Georgia, we've been able to take on singular fights and get a lot of momentum and win. The problem for a long time has been that, once it's won, philanthropists and politicians say, 'Okay, done! Educational reform, check the box. We can move on now.'"

That strategy, says Rhee, allows her opponents to return later and roll back the individual wins, picking them off one at a time. To counter those retrenchments, StudentsFirst is running a rolling offense, constantly advancing on a broad range of initiatives. "This has to be a sustained effort over a 5- to 10-year period to get *all* 37 of these policies put in place. It's not just situational fights. It's a comprehensive strategy, and it's going to take a long time, and you've got to be in for the long haul."

In its first three years, StudentsFirst has been ineffective in some states but has strung up clear victories in others. "In the 17 states where we're active," smiles Rhee, "we've passed more than 115 policies. If you read our policy agenda, you'll know these are not soft policies. They have been thought of as extraordinarily controversial for a long time. We've helped to push some important ballot initiatives, like the ones in Cleveland and in Georgia, and we've also helped to defend places like Michigan where the unions were trying to roll back some very strong reforms. Finally, we supported more than 100 political candidates in the 2012 election—with a win rate of about 75 percent."

StudentsFirst isn't the only game in town. Some other organizations are viewed as just as effective in shepherding legislation and changing opinions. These include Stand for Children, the strongest state chapters of 50CAN, Democrats for Education Reform, the American Federation for Children, and others sketched below in the subsection "A menu of other advocates."

State-level advocacy

Because most charter policies are set by state legislatures, all states with a charter law (and many of those without one) have at least one statewide organization dedicated to educating policymakers and the public about the need for stronger charter policies. Some are independent nonprofits governed by parents, community and business leaders, or education reformers. Others are membership-based "associations" or "leagues" of charter schools with a strong emphasis on policy issues. Throughout the years, these organizations have successfully led efforts like these:

• Lifting or eliminating caps on the number of charter schools allowed in a state

- Expanding the range of bodies that can authorize schools in a state
- Increasing funding for charter schools
- Opening up access to facilities financing
- Reducing restrictions on charter school autonomy
- Repelling efforts by opponents to weaken charter laws

Private philanthropies that cannot legally advocate on a large scale *can* fund these groups that include lobbying as part of their work. A pioneer in this area was the Gates Family Foundation of Colorado (not affiliated with the Bill & Melinda Gates Foundation). More than a decade ago, when charters were just nascent in their state and most others, Gates invested in a one-day conference that brought in crucial players involved in passage of the Minnesota and California charter laws. According to one Gates Family Foundation officer, that conference "lit a fire under several Colorado policymakers and educators." Within six months, charter schools were legal in the state.

Gates went on to provide vital seed funding for the Colorado League of Charter Schools, which became an influential statewide advocate. It has won policy victories in expanding facilities-financing for charters, among other vital goals. As of the 2013-14 school year, Colorado has almost 200 charter schools, which enroll more than 10 percent of all public school students in the state. In addition to things like technical assistance, training, and lots of information, the Colorado League supplies member schools with a list of legislative priorities and help in getting important policies enacted.

Another donor that has nurtured state-level advocates is the Chicago-based Joyce Foundation. They provided multiple grants to the Illinois Network of Charter Schools that allowed information about that state's charters to be disseminated to key public and policymaking audiences. Along with practical services like a teacher job fair and a service for matching board members to schools, the Illinois Network's 145 schools get a range of advocacy assists. These range from published profiles that celebrate the achievements of charter school graduates to lobbying the legislature and governor's office on behalf of its members. In 2009, the network helped pass a law that doubled the number of charter schools permitted to operate in the state.

The California Charter Schools Association, the largest such organization with 1,130 member schools, is another effective state advocate that has been built up with philanthropic funding. Like others it provides useful help like financial, legal, and instructional training. But its most vital role is to keep school leaders engaged in legislation and policies that affect charter schools. Among its creative contributions is an online Legislative Advocacy Toolkit created to assist parents in contacting elected officials. The Association is also conducting a legal battle, funded by donors, to enforce Proposition 39, a successful ballot measure in California that requires local school districts to provide charter schools with facilities that are "reasonably equivalent" to those which students would enjoy if they were attending a conventional district school.

The Texas Charter Schools Association is also heavily involved in litigation and advocacy. Its current priorities including lifting charter school caps and improving the financing of charter schools. The association was founded with support from the Dell, Walton, and Gates foundations.

The Arizona Charter Schools Association is one of the most active and successful state advocates. With 17 percent of all students in the state now enrolled in charters (and rising), Arizona has a constituency for charter-friendly policies that has gotten too big to brush aside. The state association has been active in promoting excellent charter schools for both low-income and middle-class communities (Arizona has done much better than other states at producing some schools that serve the latter neighborhoods).

Not all state charter associations are equally effective. Some tend to prioritize membership numbers over school quality. This can cause them to take neutral stands on measures that would raise academic demands, tighten authorizer scrutiny of charters, or close poor-performing schools. Donors can play a role in strengthening these groups and making their influence as salutary as possible.

A menu of other advocates

Philanthropists fighting to make sure their investments in charter schools are backed up by intelligent and supportive public policies will need to join forces with a range of organizations, employing varied tactics in different places at specific times. Along with the national and state groups discussed above, here is an illustrative selection of other advocates that donors might partner with, depending on the kind of policy intervention needed.

- The donor-supported National Alliance for Public Charter Schools exists to increase public support and political understanding of charter schools. Its Washington, D.C., operation toils on a wide range of policy and regulatory issues. It also has a special state advocacy and support team that focuses intensely on topics that come up in high-priority states. Its affiliated arm, the Alliance of Public Charter School Attorneys, provides guidance on legal and courthouse strategies. The alliance aims to ensure that parents, the press, and policymakers see chartering as a powerful and permanent improvement in public education.

- Stand for Children is a 501(c)(4) organization that labors to elect public officials who support education reform and wider school options. It maintains a local presence in 11 states. In 2011, it was instrumental in supporting a bill in Indiana that resulted in more comprehensive teacher evaluations, a performance-based compensation model, and an end to "last in, first out" layoff policies. It also played a part in helping reelect a pro-reform school board majority in Denver by reaching 21,000 voters via phone banks and canvassing.

- The American Federation for Children is a 501(c)(4) with offices across the country that advocates for school choice. It has a special focus on school vouchers and scholarship tax credit programs that vulnerable children can use to attend private or religious schools, but it also promotes and defends charter schools. The group was founded in 2010 and is led by education donor Betsy DeVos. It works closely with the Alliance for School Choice, a 501(c)(3) which provides guidance, strategies, quality-enhancement, and growth support for schools of choice.

- The Center for Education Reform, based in D.C., advocates for policy change on national, state, and local levels. It defends school choice, works to advance the charter sector, and challenges the inefficiencies of the education establishment. It offers weekly e-news updates, communications training, and networking meetings to support charter schools in particular. Among its other publications, the center rates state charter laws, compiles an annual directory of charter schools across the nation, formulates a "parent power index" showing how much influence families have on education policy in their state, and scores media stories on K-12 education for accuracy and fairness.

- 50CAN (the 50-State Campaign for Achievement Now) grew out of an organization in Connecticut that used a paired strategy of 501(c)(3) research plus 501(c)(4) lobbying and voter engagement. The Connecticut successes included lifting that state's cap on charter school numbers, increasing charter-school operating grants, securing $50 million in funding for charter school facilities, implementing teacher evaluations based on student achievement, and opening the Nutmeg State's first alternative pathway for principal certification. These successes led to offices in additional states. By 2015, 25 state CANs are slated to be up and running.
- CEE-Trust, funded by donors including the Gates Foundation, is a national network of more than 30 city organizations (nonprofits, philanthropists, mayors' offices, etc.) that cooperate on policy changes to improve U.S. education. The group does some advocacy, for instance regularly calling for fairer funding of charter schools, but it also does much more—sponsoring working groups on topics like reforming school governance, incubating charters, encouraging blended learning, producing publications.
- The U.S. Chamber of Commerce, speaking on behalf of businesses nationwide, sometimes advocates for charter schools as a means to ensure future economic growth. "Public charter schools are without a doubt one of the nation's most promising efforts to produce more great public schools," says Arthur Rothkopf of the chamber. "We must do everything we can to increase the supply."
- The Black Alliance for Educational Options (BAEO) is a national organization with local affiliates in seven cities and states. BAEO and its local offices exist to advocate for the expansion of educational choices, and to empower black families by providing them with information about their schooling options. Using media and old-fashioned organizing, BAEO actively builds community support for policies friendly to charters and other school alternatives.
- Democrats for Education Reform includes (c)(3), (c)(4), and PAC arms that support high academic standards, innovation, and accountability in education—including high-quality charter schools. "People ask us all the time why we can't

call ourselves '*Everyone* for Education Reform,'" chuckles DFER's Joseph Williams. "Our answer is that, historically, education reform has faced problems within the Democratic Party. We need to get the Democrats caught up. Then we can have a bipartisan working environment." Contributions to DFER come from individuals like William Ackman, Boykin Curry, Charles Ledley, John Petry, and Whitney Tilson on the political side, and its (c)(3) operations are supported by foundations like Broad. DFER has promoted a bill to lift the cap on the number of charter schools in New York state, and hosted rallies and events on behalf of charter schools across the nation.

- EdVoice is a lobbying group in California with a budget of about $1.5 million a year that aims to balance the influence of teacher unions in certain legislative fights. California businessmen who donate to charter schools provided the initial funding. "They got together and said, 'Hey, it's time to put some political muscle behind our education-reform ideals,'" explains Scott Hamilton, former CEO of the KIPP Foundation.

- Parent Revolution, directed by Ben Austin, is another California group focused even more tightly on the Los Angeles region. It brings together parents to press for change in the Los Angeles Unified School District. It runs an informative website with information about current campaigns, an action handbook, and an online sign-up to receive e-mails about upcoming events. The group has promoted the so-called "parent trigger" that allows families to force change at persistently failing public schools.

- New Schools for New Orleans is a very effective advocate in the city that leads the nation in experimentation with charter schools. NSNO sponsors public and parent information initiatives—including print and online versions of the *New Orleans Parents' Guide to Public Schools*—which help ensure that parents and community members understand the charter model and are aware of their educational options. NSNO has also sponsored radio advertisements to spread the word about charter schools, and helped create a local office dedicated to providing parents with tools and information that allow them to advocate for themselves when choosing a school.

Is eroding monopolies the ultimate policy reform?

"Fifteen years ago, everybody was really excited about how the conventional public schools in Seattle were improving themselves. Now you never hear about Seattle." That's the voice of Reed Hastings, former president of the California State Board of Education, founder of Netflix, and a major donor to school reform. "What's happening is that instead of improving, school districts are just oscillating. With a thousand large school districts in the nation, there are always some that are improving, and we say 'See? It can work.' But if you look over the long term, nothing has really changed conventional school districts."

Hastings argues that until all schools in America are spun off into autonomous governance, "we're doomed. We get excited about the work that Joel Klein did in New York, the work that Kaya Henderson has done in D.C. Those are really good for the decade we're in, but over the years you just don't see continuity. The problem is the school board or the mayor changes, and so you don't get a chance to sustain excellence. What district got fixed 30 years ago and stayed fixed?"

Hastings, who has been a major progenitor of charter schools and also served on the board of the California Charter Schools Association, calls charter schools "the best opportunity we have" not just for their ability to deliver better education to the kids attending them but because they provide "competition for school districts" that will force mainline schools to innovate, hire and fire better, use technology more wisely, and otherwise elevate their performance. "It's what you pioneer with charter schools that will drive improvements generally." That's why he devotes "half" of his education philanthropy today to "political reform" that will create more room for entrepreneurial schools like charters.

Other major donors have had a similar insight. Noting the dramatic expansion of the charter sector in the District of Columbia over the last decade, philanthropist Katherine Bradley observes that "this growth has created huge pressure on our conventional D.C. public schools to get better. It has been remarkable watching the change in our district schools in concert with the proliferation of our charters."

The deepest payoff from advocacy on behalf of charter schools could thus actually be to transform conventional schools.

The deepest payoff from advocacy on behalf of charter schools could thus actually be to transform conventional schools. Donors who use policy activism to defend charters may ultimately plant the innovations they are pioneering—like greater flexibility and accountability for teachers, the more powerful principal role, a longer school day, and so forth—in many other places as well. This is a wonderful bonus, because no matter how much money and energy philanthropy devotes to spreading charter schools, a majority of children will never get a shot at a seat in a charter in the near term.

The logical next step for activist donors, thinkers like Neerav Kingsland and Andy Smarick suggest, should be to encourage public questioning of the old notion of the school district itself. "Can we reinvent what public education looks like? That seems to be the next phase," argues Kingsland. "Funders should actively talk about the idea that it could work for whole districts to be made up solely of charter schools" (as New Orleans has already nearly achieved, and as smaller districts in Michigan and Georgia are also doing).

"The traditional public school system in large urban areas cannot be fixed," says Smarick, author of *The Urban School System of the Future*. "For great results, it must be *replaced*—by a new 'system of schools' governed by the practices of chartering. Today's ecosystem of charters has shown that the government need not be the exclusive operator of public schools. A wide array of organizations can deliver a public education in a schools marketplace that decentralizes power, delivers variety, continually innovates and shuts down failures, and turns citizens into customers able to exercise choice. Urban governments must shift into the business of managing portfolios of schools operated by others. And we should stop seeing chartering as a 'sector'—it should become the system through which all urban public education is governed in the future."

By producing new thinking like this, charter school success itself has become a driver of new policy. At a minimum, it pushes policymakers toward neutrality on the question of whether families should educate their children at conventional schools, charters, or some other school of choice. If the logic of charter school success eventually played out fully, the result could be deep structural change of America's monolithic public-school systems that have so long resisted any significant remake. At that point it would be no exaggeration to refer to the charter school movement as a "revolution."

Solving Special Operational Issues

Operating outside of state and district bureaucracies gives a charter school the chance to forge an ambitious mission and then be highly inventive in aligning its day-to-day activities with those goals. Autonomy comes at a price though. The more independently a charter school operates, the more it is cut off from the practical supports offered by established educational systems. For district schools, having a facility is a given. The central office takes care of services like accounting, transportation, food service, security, employee benefits, regulatory compliance, purchasing of equipment and curricula, annual testing, and staff training. Governance is handled by the district superintendent and board of education.

Charter schools have to manage all of that, and more, on their own. Few charters would trade their freedom of operation in order to obtain those services, and if they did, most would lose their performance edge. Yet the lack of logistical support that many charters feel can create heavy operational burdens and hamper their ability to function as effectively as they might.

Some examples of a few of the practical responsibilities that can dog charter operators today:

- Charter school leaders sometimes spend a lot of time dealing with back-office issues (financial management, supply purchases, state reporting).
- Special-education requirements apply to charter schools, as they do to all public schools, pulling charters into complicated and expensive regulatory compliance.
- The oversight boards required for each charter are legal entities that carry fiduciary and statutory demands. Keeping up with these can eat time and resources that principals would rather put into improving instruction.
- Perhaps most taxing are the demands of acquiring and maintaining facilities. At last count, only 15 states plus D.C. provided charter schools with *any* financial compensation for the cost of facilities. Most charter schools are thus forced to take a significant chunk of the money that states apportion them for instructional expenses (an amount that already averages much less than what conventional schools get per child) and devote that to their building.

When you ask charter school founders and operators about the toughest problems they face, financing facilities regularly tops the list. The costs of buying land, erecting a large building, or renovating an existing structure can be prohibitive for an enterprise that doesn't yet have any income stream. Since charter schools can go out of business or be shut down for poor performance, lenders often see them as a risky investment. Exacerbating this is the fact that charters are often first ventures for those who start them up, while most founders are educators without a lot of business or real-estate experience. Financiers charge a premium to cover these perceived risks, and charter schools end up paying carrying costs heavier than those of regular school districts.

While financing a facility remains very difficult for many charter schools, it has become somewhat less lonely and expensive than it used to be. The Local Initiatives Support Corporation has surveyed dozens of nonprofits that began offering financial assistance for charter school buildings over the last decade. By mid-2012, their research showed, a total of 583 facilities costing $6.4 billion had been helped with bonding. The assisting groups were partly encouraged to enter this arena by the U.S. Department of Education's Credit Enhancement Program, which assists nonprofits who develop such programs.

The best long-term solution would be for state, federal, and local education authorities to treat charter schools like other public schools when it comes to facilities. This could involve allowing them access to public financing and bonding, folding an allotment for building costs

> There are many superb schools operating out of strip malls, closed big-box stores, converted warehouses. Don't get hung up on fancy facilities.

into the per-pupil payments made to charter schools, and allocating closed or surplus schools to charter operators. Putting charters and conventional schools on equal footing in this area should be an important priority within the advocacy work discussed in Chapter 5. Groups like StudentsFirst and the various state charter associations are emphasizing this problem, and may get traction if sustained in their efforts.

In the meantime, there are growing numbers of ways that donors can help talented charter founders and operators jump the difficult hurdle of acquiring a home for their school. We'll sketch several options in the first sections of this chapter.

Giving charter schools direct support for facilities
Building grants to charter schools are one simple way for givers to ease facilities pain. Or something more involved can be undertaken—like the

donation of a building directly to a charter school operator, or its lease at a low cost. The Longwood Foundation of Delaware, for example, worked with Bank of America to turn an office building the bank no longer needed into the Community Education Building. Along with other philanthropic and civic partners, Longwood provided management and financing to remake this space into a facility for high-performing charter schools and community organizations, which will eventually serve some 2,000 of Wilmington's children.

Philanthropists may also offer loans or loan guarantees. To make charter schools a more attractive investment for lenders, several donors put foundation backing behind the mortgage debts of one or more charter schools. By placing funds into a reserve account or simply signing a guarantee letter, funders can provide lenders with a degree of security that encourages their lending and reduces interest rates. This is known as "credit enhancement" because it boosts a school's standing to operate in the private financial marketplace.

Interventions like these where philanthropists act almost like investors or banks rather than simply giving donations are sometimes referred to as "program-related investments." Foundations can sometimes put portions of their endowments into PRIs, with the expectation of getting their principal back, and perhaps also some modest return on their money. Several donors—the Walton Family Foundation and the Ewing Marion Kauffman Foundation, for instance—have been making PRIs to help charter schools acquire useable campuses. When loans get repaid, or rent or interest installments are returned, the giver can recycle that money into additional PRIs for other operators. In this way, a given sum of capital can get multiple uses in kickstarting buildings and new schools.

Donors should be aware that many of the best charter operators are exceptionally frugal with physical facilities. Most would rather put discretionary funds into teachers, curriculum, or technology, so charter schools are often quite spartan in their physical plants. There are many superb schools operating out of strip malls, closed big-box stores, converted warehouses or call centers, old tortilla factories, and former car dealerships. Many do without full gyms, auditoriums, cafeterias, large playing fields, or decorative flourishes. Schools need not reside in classical structures to have great academic results. Many creative school founders have improvised unusual real-estate solutions, and donors who aim to help with the facilities crunch should encourage school leaders to research the workarounds already pioneered by others.

While in many older Northeastern cities there are vacant buildings, and often even vacant schools, that can be repurposed efficiently, there are other places and times when new construction is the best choice. In newer cities in the South and West that are less dense and have cheaper land, it may be smarter and even less expensive to build from scratch, yielding exactly the campus a school wants at a modest cost. In short, there is no single best way to house a school.

Several charter networks have perfected fast, no-frills construction, including BASIS, Carpe Diem, National Heritage Academies, and Rocketship. BASIS has been putting up modern steel and glass school buildings in Arizona at a cost of around $8 million including the land. That is less than *half* the cost of a typical school built in the Phoenix area. They do it by prefabricating the building in Texas, trucking to the site in pieces, and assembling it in just a few months. *Education Next* reporter June Kronholz recently visited a new BASIS school building and described some of their secrets of cost control.

> There's no cafeteria or library. Floors are polished cement. The ductwork is exposed. Theater and orchestra audiences assemble on the parking lot—a garage door in front of them opens into the performing-arts room. I noticed overhead projectors and a cart of laptop computers, but there's no technology lab.

"Of course if proscenium stages and audiovisual equipment made a difference in student learning," Kronholz concludes, "the U.S. wouldn't be struggling to keep up with the international average."

In some places, the quickest and most efficient way a donor can help a charter school find a physical home is to help arrange a facilities-sharing agreement with the local school district. Even as charter schools across the country clamor for more space, many districts are facing declining enrollments and closing underused campuses. Where local leaders are able to overcome the suspicions that often exist between district officials and charters, charters have frequently ended up housed in closed district schools, or even in one wing or floor of a district school whose remaining space continues to be used by a conventional public school. This has happened in New York City, D.C., Denver, Philadelphia, Chicago, Atlanta, and elsewhere.

When political winds shift, this occasionally leaves charters exposed. In New York City, for instance, mayor Bill de Blasio has voiced harsh skepticism toward the previous policy of sharing unused schools with charters (even though charters and conventional schools are both public institutions serving interchangeable populations). Where leaders are cooperative, however, school handoffs or space sharing can be win-win scenarios.

One example can be seen in Philadelphia, where the school district is working closely with the local Mastery Charter Schools network. Mastery has agreed to take over operation of some of the district's poorest performing schools, and then convert them to charter status. One advantage of this arrangement is that it typically allows the charter to use the district facility in that neighborhood.

To upgrade the inherited school to meet its needs, Mastery obtains its own construction loan from the Reinvestment Fund, a community-development group based in the region that has paid for (among other things) the facilities for 36,000 charter students. Mastery, a lean organization free of the bureaucratic strictures that encumber any construction undertaken by the school district, makes the building improvements quickly and comparatively cheaply. Then the district buys the improvements back and gives Mastery a long-term lease for the facility. This allows Mastery to obtain a custom facility at low cost—and keeps valuable public facilities from going to waste.

In some places, cooperation on facilities becomes a foot-in-the-door for wider collaboration between charters and districts. One such example comes from Columbus, Ohio, where the Fordham Foundation and a coalition of more than 30 local businesses helped broker and pay for an arrangement where a KIPP school was able to lease a closed campus from the Columbus Public Schools. In exchange, the district got to incorporate the impressive achievement scores of those KIPP students into its overall accountability ratings—a strong incentive for the district to play ball.

Even as charter schools across the country clamor for more space, many districts are facing declining enrollments and closing underused campuses. Property transfers and space sharing can help both sides.

In the Houston region, an interesting effort called the Sky Partnership began in the 2012-13 school year. The Spring Branch Independent School District invited KIPP and YES Prep to start operating a few grades right within some of the district's underperforming schools. The charter operators will add more grades every year, eventually taking over their campus entirely. The goal is not only better outcomes for the children in those schools, but also "shared learning" which will allow the district to absorb some of the school culture of successful charters with the aim of raising achievement in its own schools.

Giving to organizations that help charters find buildings

Philanthropists who want to attack the facilities crisis on more than a one-school-at-a-time basis can contribute to regional and national organizations that have sprung up over the last decade or so to help charter operators obtain space. These groups specialize in either providing facility financing directly to the schools or helping them obtain outside financing, and many of them are quite nimble. These entities enjoy significant philanthropic funding.

Building Hope, for instance, is a nonprofit based in Washington, D.C. It relies on support from the Walton Family Foundation, the Sallie Mae Fund, and other donors to orchestrate below-market loans and lease guarantees that allow charter schools to acquire, construct, or renovate school facilities. Since its inception in 2003, the organization has provided 30 loan- and lease-guarantees which have enabled real-estate transactions worth over $230 million.

Some other examples of similar organizations:

- Low Income Investment Fund (which has financed 69,000 school seats)
- Local Initiatives Support Corporation (spun out of the Ford Foundation, this is one of the oldest and largest such organizations, though charter schools are only one portion of its development activity)
- Charter Schools Development Corporation (the only one of these organizations focused solely on charter school facilities; operates nationally)
- Housing Partnership Network (an alliance of community-development nonprofits located all across the country)

- Reinvestment Fund (mentioned in the Philly case above)
- Illinois Facilities Fund
- New Jersey Community Capital
- Self-Help Credit Union (North Carolina based but operating in other states too)
- Raza Development Fund (Hispanic oriented)

There are also organizations that go beyond just financing and sometimes also help charter leaders find, renovate, design, build, or lease buildings. These groups are often able to secure better terms than a new charter school could on its own, and they also add development expertise. Sometimes they assume the facilities burden in toto, freeing the school's staff and board to focus on educating students.

Civic Builders is an example of one of these "development" intermediaries. It is a New York City-based nonprofit that finds, purchases, and refurbishes buildings, and then leases them at affordable rates to charter schools. With support from the NewSchools Venture Fund, the Bill & Melinda Gates Foundation, the Michael & Susan Dell Foundation, and the Annie E. Casey Foundation, Civic Builders allows charter schools to focus on academics rather than the ordeal of navigating the New York City real estate market.

Somewhat similar work is done across the state of California by a real-estate development nonprofit called Pacific Charter School Development. Starting with around $50 million of initial equity contributed by the NewSchools Venture Fund and the Ahmanson, Gates, Broad, Walton, Weingart, and Ralph M. Parsons foundations, PCSD has revolved that money into a total of $353 million of investments in 45 charter school buildings, creating 19,000 student seats. Starting with tax-advantaged debt financing, PCSD provides facilities consulting and construction management that finishes buildings very efficiently. Most completed projects are eventually sold at cost to their school clients, with the proceeds funneled back into another development elsewhere. The organization has particularly partnered with six of the nation's leading charter chains, but with dedicated funding from the Walton Family Foundation it has also made special efforts to work with high-quality smaller "mom and pop" charter operators, who often need facilities help even more than their bigger brothers.

The Charter School Growth Fund has assembled a Revolving Facilities Loan Fund that offers existing school operators short- and medium-term financing for facilities, allowing them to grow their networks of schools without scrambling every time they want to acquire a new property. The revolving fund accepts program-related investments from foundations and then combines them with funding from more traditional lenders like CitiBank. It also helps stable school chains find more permanent financing like bonds or traditional loans. This allows the schools to pay off their CSGF bridge loans, and those funds are then recycled back into a speedy school expansion by some other charter operator.

Though it is a for-profit operation, unlike the three groups just mentioned, the Canyon-Agassi Charter School Facilities Fund is another entity that philanthropists operating in this area should know about and learn from. Former tennis star Andre Agassi became a supporter of the charter-school movement after he founded his own charter school for children in Las Vegas. In 2011 he pooled funds with Canyon Capital Realty Advisors to create the Canyon-Agassi fund, which also received anchor investments from Citi, Intel Capital, and the Ewing Marion Kauffman Foundation.

The fund is positioned to build half a billion dollars worth of charter school infrastructure over the next few years. This will create new slots for up to 50,000 students on 100 campuses. As this book is being written in 2014 the fund is constructing its 24th campus—a brand new $7 million school on a three-acre site in Nashville that will be run by Rocketship Education.

Canyon-Agassi's partnership with Rocketship illustrates its pioneering formula. The fund uses its own money and its own site-selection, design, construction, and finance specialists to erect structures and playgrounds to the exact specifications of Rocketship (or other school operator). It delivers turn-key properties, relieving school leaders of all burdens of raising capital, planning, and managing construction in new markets. In exchange, the school executes a long-term lease and pledges annual payments, as soon as the school starts operating, of up to 20 percent of the per-pupil reimbursements it receives from the local public school authority. In the early years when schools are only partially enrolled, Canyon-Agassi thus subsidizes the leases. As schools become big enough, they cover their own annual rent. By paying 100 percent of project costs and stepping down rents in the beginning, Canyon-Agassi bridges new schools over the financial strains of their crucial startup years. Once the school reaches operational maturity—typically between its third and sixth year—it can choose to execute an option to purchase its building at a predetermined, affordable price. Philanthropic funders sometimes assist these purchases.

If this sort of practical help can be expanded over the next decade, then both the individuals and grassroots groups who want to start stand-alone schools and the charter school networks that want to expand their footprint will find their mission much easier. Philanthropists who help solve this operational obstacle may thus tip the scales in favor of growth and expansion. And charter leaders will be freed to focus on their most important work of educating students.

Handling back-office services more efficiently

The back-office activities that take place behind the scenes at schools are essential to keeping teaching and learning humming. Payroll, accounting, pensions, and other aspects of personnel and financial management are important practical components that need to be managed carefully. Information technology is now a big responsibility at all schools. Food service is not to be overlooked, particularly given that many charters predominantly serve students who qualify for subsidized school meals. Transportation can be complicated at charter schools, which generally accept students by lottery from across a city, rather than just serving one immediate neighborhood.

Charter schools either have to provide these services themselves or find outside vendors. "Doing it yourself" saps valuable time and energy, while the market for vendors can be difficult to navigate, leaving some charter leaders without easy solutions. Funders across the country have applied several strategies to help with these operations challenges.

Some donors—like the New York City-based Tiger Foundation— have provided direct support to schools. They set up training programs covering back-office services where they see many grantees needing help. Much of the technical assistance they have created themselves.

Another route for donors is to fund local or regional charter support organizations that specialize in providing these services to charter schools. The New York City Charter School Center was launched in 2004 with support from the Robertson, Pumpkin, Clark, and Robin Hood foundations (and with the backing of Joel Klein, then chancellor of the New York City school system). It offers help with data management, teacher training, facility maintenance, and other practical aspects of operations. New Schools for New Orleans serves a similar role for the charter schools in its city.

Funders have similarly built up the California Charter Schools Association to provide business services to its members across California. Offerings include insurance policies, startup assistance, leadership training, and access to a vendor network to which day-to-day needs can be efficiently outsourced. Similar resource offerings through charter school associations exist in almost every state, though not all are currently offering services as thorough and wide-ranging as California's. The Marcus Foundation has helped build up the back-office assistance offered by the Georgia Charter Schools Association, the Kauffman Foundation has aided the Missouri Charter Public School Association toward similar ends. Many more examples could be added.

ExED is part of a category of nonprofits that focus completely and solely on providing business-management services to charters. It has aided more than 100 schools over its 12-year life, helping not only with things like payroll and benefit processing, accounting, and

> Charters always need legal advice on a range of issues. This is an area where philanthropy can make a big difference.

audit, but also compliance with today's thicket of state and federal regulations, as well as assistance in securing affordable facilities. ExED bills itself as the "CFO" for each of its client schools. Thanks to philanthropic support, ExED's clients never pay more than 5 percent of their public revenues for these services.

At a minimum, charter schools can draw on the useful business information now provided through the newsletters, websites, and workshops of various resource centers, member associations, and support organizations. Most of these groups also advocate for public policies that would make operations easier for charter schools. And many offer individualized technical assistance, answering specific questions or connecting a school with specialists who can.

These support groups, and the donors who fund them, are also zeroing in on solving more specific infrastructure challenges. How does a school improve its special-ed services? Build a strong board? Integrate technology into the curriculum in the most intelligent ways? Establish fundraising operations? Conduct annual assessments? Organize professional development for teachers?

One other crucial area where many small charter schools want help is legal services. "Charters always need legal advice on a range of issues," notes Christopher Nelson of the Fisher Fund. "This is an area where philanthropy can make a big difference, and one that is frequently overlooked."

The Atlantic Legal Foundation is a legal nonprofit that advises, educates, and represents charter schools (among its other missions). Their charter school advocacy program publishes a series of state-specific legal guides, written by nationally known labor law attorneys. The foundation will also assist charter schools in court, free of charge. It offers "friend of the court" briefs that focus on broad policy concerns that have not been developed adequately by plaintiffs and defendants. In addition to offering legal advice itself at reduced rates or no charge, it will also link charter school leaders with private-sector lawyers able and willing to provide representation.

One issue for the future: Some entrepreneurs have been asking if back-office services could be provided to charter schools easily and in bulk via the Internet, on a statewide basis or even nationally. This could be an opening for pioneering philanthropy or even for savvy businesspeople. For now, help with back-office services tends to be provided on fairly local and case-by-case bases.

Meeting specialized needs

The operational challenges we've discussed up to now are faced by all charter schools. There are also more specific operational issues that will loom larger or smaller depending on the particular school, its mission, and who attends. These include things like providing particular health or poverty services in neighborhoods where that is necessary, or special-ed and English-learning services (common to many charters). There are charter schools focused specifically on "alternative" students—dropout risks, those with children, those with behavior problems, those seeking technical education; obviously these pose their own operational demands. There are also rising new operational questions like how to teach good character (an interest in many charter schools), and how to shift schools toward blended learning (using computers for more individualized learning and redeploying teachers as small-group instructors). In the remainder of this chapter we'll briefly look at a few of these issues.

In today's educational jargon, "wraparound services" are various kinds of assistance offered to students and families that go beyond the normal scope of schooling. These include health care, counseling, and other social services. This is a tricky area. It is sometimes argued that it is hard for education to begin if disturbances in family or personal life are keeping a child from focusing in the classroom. On the other hand, turning a school into a centralized hub responsible for feeding, nursing, nurturing, and acculturating the child is a kind of mission creep almost sure to interfere with teaching, and to dramatically raise the complexity and cost of school operations.

Some donors have tried to help charter schools thread this needle. For example, the Richard M. Fairbanks Foundation, the Health Foundation of Greater Indianapolis, and others in that city have supported the work of Learning Well, a nonprofit that places nurses in many charter schools in Indianapolis. Fairbanks has contributed more than $7 million to fund nursing positions and school-based clinics in all the charter schools across the city.

Promise Academy is a charter school chain in New York City that integrates wraparound services into its campuses. These schools are part of the Harlem Children's Zone, 100 blocks of traditionally low-income neighborhoods where a massive philanthropic effort is under way aimed at reducing poverty. Elements include free, school-based health centers, an Asthma Initiative, a Healthy Living Initiative, and programs aimed at strengthening families and reducing the need for foster care.

Donors interested in religious and spiritual education have supported religious training as another supplemental wraparound service. Seton Partners, for example, helps establish rigorous after-school programs that combine academics, exercise, and faith instruction, all available to charter school students at no or low cost should they and their parents elect to participate. This allows families who cannot afford a private religious school a chance to receive, on a voluntary basis, religious education for their children.

Charters, as public schools, are open to all students, including those with disabilities, so special education is a major operational need at nearly all charter schools. A 2012 report from the U.S. Government Accountability Office found that 8 percent of all charter school students were receiving special-education services. (In conventional public schools the average was 11 percent.) The costs of complying with myriad federal and state special-ed laws can be daunting, particularly for small schools and schools in states where reimbursements to charter schools are much lower than those to convention schools.

There are prominent examples of charter schools having success with special-education students. Granada Hills is a very large (4,300 students) charter high school in Los Angeles that gets high performance not only out of its overall student body but also from its special-education pupils specifically. Technological interventions has been a big part of their formula. Aspire, one of the largest charter school networks, has a reputation for serving special-ed students well. Collegiate Academies is a group of three charter schools in New Orleans that achieves consistently higher test results among its 99 percent minority, 93 percent poor enrollees than the average school in Louisiana. It does this while fully 18 percent of its students are enrolled in special-education classes.

> A five-person team bird-dogs students with warnings, text messages, phone calls, and home visits to keep them from becoming truant.

Just the same, special-ed is an area where charters (like conventional schools) sometimes struggle. "We need to place a much greater focus on helping charter schools figure out how to better serve and reach out to students with special needs," says Nina Rees of the National Alliance for Public Charter Schools. One way donors have pitched in is by helping schools form special-education cooperatives—in which they join forces to ensure that they are providing a quality education to students with disabilities and complying with all applicable requirements.

The Annie E. Casey Foundation provided early funding for the District of Columbia Special Education Cooperative, and current funders include the Moriah Fund and the Morris & Gwendolyn Cafritz Foundation. Through this cooperative, schools have access to technical assistance and teacher training for special-ed. They can share staff and make joint arrangements with special-ed contractors. The cooperative helps schools get reimbursements through Medicaid.

A similar cooperative exists in New Orleans, called the SUNS Center. In addition to providing day-to-day services it manages a leadership academy that trains special-ed administrators for charter schools. These cooperatives borrow techniques from the regional cooperatives that school districts have utilized for some time to keep the costs of special-ed services manageable.

To improve special-education performance in charter schools nationwide, the Walton Family Foundation and other philanthropists helped create the National Center for Special Education in Charter Schools. This organization highlights excellent programs, develops and disseminates workable solutions, and informs policymaking. It also communicates with authorizers and legislators on special-ed services in charter schools.

Then there are so-called "alternative" charter schools, which provide customized education for students who have not succeeded in traditional schools. Some of these students are returning after dropping out. Others are young parents, have a criminal history, or need to schedule study around a part- or full-time job. These populations pose enormous challenges, and have often led to lowered academic standards and criticism of alternative schools as "diploma mills" that allow students to get by on minimal effort, leaving them ill prepared for gainful employment or higher education after graduation.

With their increased autonomy and flexibility in scheduling, staffing, and other operational details, it is hoped that charter schools might have more potential than district schools to succeed with some of these difficult students. Three pioneering charter schools in this arena are the School for Integrated Academics and Technologies (SIATech), the Phoenix Charter School, and the Excel Centers. Each is constructed to belie the "diploma mill" rap via high standards and extra work.

SIATech operates charter schools in California, Arkansas, Arizona, Florida, and New Mexico. All of the campuses adjoin Jobs Corps centers administering a federal program that offers occupational training to high-school dropouts. Through a mix of online and in-person instruction, SIATech helps dropouts earn a full high-school diploma instead of a GED. The average student enrolled in their program makes two years' worth of academic gains in literacy and math in just one year's time. And because this academic work is matched with technical training from the Jobs Corps site, graduates emerge with much improved employability.

Phoenix Charter Academy, located in Chelsea, Massachusetts, is another charter that has had success with difficult students (54 percent former dropouts, 14 percent involved with the courts, 13 percent parents, 29 percent with special disability curricula). Every attendee is given an individual course plan without any set time parameters. Progress is measured not in years or grade level but according to proven mastery of the curriculum. The school has a strict culture, a longer school day, a longer school year, and high standards—including AP classes and college-class dual-enrollment options. It also offers extraordinary social supports like on-site childcare and a dean of students who manages two on-site social workers, several Student Support Specialists who help enrollees build scholarly habits, and a five-person Attendance Transformation Team that bird-dogs students with reminders, encouragement, warnings, text messages, phone calls, and home visits to keep them from becoming truant or dropping out. Phoenix students score significantly higher on year-end state exams than *average* students at the schools they flunked out of, and a majority of graduates go on to two- and four-year colleges. Phoenix will open a second charter high school in 2014, and also manages a school in the Lawrence school district. Further expansion is planned.

The Excel Centers, founded in Indiana in 2010, are operated by Goodwill Industries' education division. They place a strong focus on career and technical training, and like the other schools mentioned here they rely on high demands, extended night and weekend hours, childcare, and support groups to help students balance school with work and often-difficult home lives. Within a short time after its launch, the original Excel Center built up a waiting list of more than 1,300 adults hoping to finish their high school educations. Seven additional centers have since opened to help meet the demand.

It isn't only among charter schools serving at-risk populations that one finds a strong focus on career and technical education. There are also lots of more mainstream charters that put special emphasis on valuable career paths. High Tech High is a California network of 11 schools with a curriculum that melds liberal arts with advanced technology education. Cornerstone Charter Health High School in Michigan lets students explore career options in health care, in partnership with the Detroit Medical Center. There are now several charter schools, including the West Michigan Aviation Academy created by philanthropist Dick DeVos, that allow students to test careers in aviation.

With money from scores of donors, three DaVinci high schools (along with an interesting K–8 school) have been created in Los Angeles to help students prepare for very specific careers. One school trains its graduates for various careers in design (architecture, product design, graphics, etc.). Another school is focused on engineering and science. The newest school to open provides special instruction in communications, and includes an option of attending a fifth year which will yield not only a high-school diploma but also a college associate's degree, or major installment toward a bachelor's.

Offering a rounded education

Good charter schools will use their flexibility to sometimes pioneer new methods and subjects of teaching, and new ways of tracking student knowledge and skill. This kind of social invention can have great value, but also be challenging to figure out. Both are good reasons for philanthropists to offer support.

Take testing, for instance. In the many charters that are beginning to explore blended learning (to be discussed more in the next section), educators are piloting more frequent, more sophisticated forms of testing that assess student knowledge every week and signal learning failures right away, rather than waiting for year-end exams to see what students have absorbed. Other charters with especially advanced curricula—like BASIS—are substituting the international PISA exam for less rigorous year-end exams, establishing a baseline for richer comparison of American schools with overseas counterparts. These sorts of innovation can have valuable overflow effects for all of American education. They can, however, be lonely and expensive journeys for charter school leaders to navigate their way through.

Another sector where charter schools are operational pioneers is in systems that inculcate and then measure important, non-academic skills, like self-control, grit, and future-oriented thinking. These qualities are being fostered as a supplement to traditional cognitive training, not as a substitute. But many charter schools start with the core idea that intellectual discovery needs to be yoked to strong character in order for the student to fully succeed. And charters are often open to unconventional methods of learning and discovery. Which is why they are deploying new styles of pedagogy like computer-assisted instruction, project-based learning, single-sex schooling, Socratic seminars, and various forms of work-connected education.

The KIPP schools are searching creatively for new character-based ways of making their students successful. Some of this was inspired by their discovery that while KIPP students are unusually successful in qualifying for and entering college, they lag middle-class students in their rates of college completion and degree attainment. Academic training alone was insufficient to get some KIPP alums over the hump of disadvantages of family life. So KIPP's leaders dug deep into research by Carol Dweck, Angela Duckworth, and other specialists and zeroed in on seven character traits that have been shown to be predictive of future personal success and fulfillment:

- Persistence and resilience ("finishing what one starts… despite obstacles")
- Zest ("approaching life with energy")
- Self-control ("regulating what one feels and does")
- Optimism ("expecting the best in the future and working to achieve it")
- Gratitude ("being aware of and thankful for opportunities")
- Social intelligence (awareness of the "motives and feelings of other people")
- Curiosity ("taking an interest…learning new things for their own sake")

Character education and moral training reinforcing these personal characteristics was woven into the school day. And in all of KIPP's charter schools each parent or guardian now receives a "character growth card" where teachers offer feedback to students across these seven traits. Students also rate themselves. Twice a year, parents, teachers, and students sit for constructive discussions of a child's ethical and humane development, and seek ways for students to burnish these essential social skills. "The kids feel like this is the coolest thing ever," says Dave Levin, who has led this work for KIPP. "They say, 'finally someone is recognizing this.'"

The efforts of KIPP leaders to improve college performance by their alums weren't limited to this character training. The school also formed partnerships with two dozen colleges, and signed formal memoranda of understanding on various steps that KIPP and the colleges would each take to support enrollees and help them complete their higher education on time. Taking this sort of long-term interest in the welfare of their students—extending years after they have left the school campus—is another charter school innovation that puts real demands of operators, while yielding valuable benefits for children.

Charter school leaders can't plow these rich new fields alone. One donor couple who are helping out are Jeff (ex-Microsoft executive) and Tricia Raikes. At another set of charter schools, their Raikes Foundation is supporting work similar to what KIPP has undertaken. A collaborative has been assembled to help schools study and then reinforce in their classrooms student qualities like tenacity and delayed gratification. "There are lots of kids out there who are lagging academically not because they aren't smart, but because they don't have the mindsets. We're trying to help them unlock their smarts with learning strategies that will let them improve in school, be ready for careers, and be successful in life," says Tricia Raikes.

Recognizing that not all children learn and communicate in the same ways, other charter schools are experimenting with rather different methods of teaching and assessing pupils. There are, for example, charter schools like MC2 in New Hampshire (funded by the QED Foundation and the Oak Foundation) that are relying heavily on "student-centered" progress measurements like major projects, pieces of artwork, oral presentations, creative writing, or song composition. The goal is to deepen students' engagement with subject matter, respect unconventional channels of learning, and get students to take ownership of their own learning process.

These sorts of innovations in educational technique and infrastructure have the potential to make charter schools much more effective. For these services to work, though, charter schools need to give them lots of management attention, resources, and follow-up assessment—operational demands which require money and talent. Done right with philanthropic partners, however, these sorts of fresh thinking and practice will separate charter schools from the pack in terms of student flourishing.

> There are lots of kids out there who are lagging academically not because they aren't smart, but because they don't have the necessary character habits.

Blending teachers and technology

Another development putting challenging operational demands on charter schools is the new blended learning instructional approach that many charters are experimenting with. Entire schools are being constructed around fresh efforts to combine the best of human and technology-enhanced instruction. Some of these are dramatic departures into new territory—producing previously unheard-of class sizes, testing methods, deployments of teachers, and uses of classroom space.

Obviously this is requiring lots of educational redesign and managerial nimbleness. It seems very likely that blended learning will be a big part of education in the future, and charter schools are far, far ahead of conventional public schools in exploring this new universe. "Blended learning is the biggest opportunity for school reformers over the next decade. And charter schools will be the innovators in this arena," says Kevin Hall of the Charter School Growth Fund. "They have the innovative spirit, flexibility in teaching force and class sizes, and ability to play with time and resources in ways that most districts aren't able to."

Christopher Nelson of the Fisher Fund agrees. "The most promising and revolutionary work in new education technologies will take place in charters, not in districts. There is some really interesting stuff going on in charter schools today. So even if it means operating on a smaller scale, the charter sector is where donors should invest." Among other things, says Neerav Kingsland of New Schools for New Orleans, blended learning could completely change the economics of public schooling—potentially reducing costs while achievement rises or stays constant.

Assisting the charter operators who are pioneering blended learning is thus vital work, and likely to have lasting effects on the future of U.S. education. Many donors are offering assistance. For example, the Joyce Foundation, Carnegie Corporation of New York, and Bill & Melinda Gates Foundation have backed an initiative run by Public Impact, called Opportunity Culture. It helps charter schools create new staffing patterns on blended learning campuses that extend the reach of excellent teachers to more students, and create career paths that could be more satisfying and remunerative for the instructor. Scores of donors like the Hume, Gates, and Broad foundations, Microsoft's philanthropic arm, and funds like Next Generation Learning Challenges, the Charter School Growth Fund, and the NewSchools Venture Fund are likewise helping school operators plan and launch new learning models enabled by technology. City-based funders like the Chicago Public Education

Fund and the CityBridge Foundation are aiding neighborhood schools as they figure out how to translate all these new ideas into day-to-day classroom operations.

Again, the definitive book on this rapidly unfolding field is *Blended Learning: A Wise Giver's Guide to Supporting Tech-assisted Teaching.* Please refer to it for many details on how philanthropists can help charter school operators meet operational challenges as they redesign schools for the twenty-first century.

Helping districts learn from charters

At the close of the previous chapter we sketched a vision of how charter schools might provoke a broad reform of American public education, altering the way conventional school districts conduct their business and touching students far beyond those enrolled in charters. The need for wholesale restructuring of public schooling is most clear in big cities. In our 50 largest urban school districts today, only 53 percent of students graduate from high school on time. Our most definitive measure, the National Assessment of Educational Progress, shows that the proportion of eighth graders who are proficient in reading is only 25 percent in New York City, 19 percent in Los Angeles, and 22 percent in Atlanta.

With little or no improvement in these poor results being seen throughout the past decade, growing numbers of observers are concluding that our urban public school districts need to be dramatically shaken up, and structured in new ways—using charter schools as the tip of the spear in our attack on educational stagnation. A small number of conventional school districts are tentatively reaching out to charters within their city boundaries and experimenting with new ways of collaborating, sharing burdens, and learning from their nimbler brethren. The extent to which charter schools are able to help large districts improve will depend on how open district leaders are, and how energetically the best ideas from charters are transferred across operational boundaries.

Philanthropists like Bill and Melinda Gates are actively trying to encourage urban school districts to establish alliances with their local charters. As mentioned toward the end of Chapter 2, their Collaboration Compacts are an effort to get school officials to put aside differences and work together to solve problems together. Areas where the Gates Foundation envisions the most cooperation include joint professional development of teachers and principals, joint implementation of Common Core standards, a universal enrollment application for all public schools, and development of standard metrics that help families make apples-to-apples comparisons of their local charter and district schools (and parochial cities as well in some cities). It is earnestly to be hoped that in at least a few of the seven cities where a Collaboration Compact is being tried most intensively—Boston, Denver, Hartford, New Orleans, New York City, Philadelphia, and Spring Branch (in metro Houston)—the school districts will go beyond the mere formalities of a truce and actually build genuine alliances with their local charter schools. The Gates Foundation has invested $27 million and extensive staff time in trying to aid that.

The Center on Reinventing Public Education, based at the university of Washington, is leading an even more thoroughgoing effort to get school districts to weave charters into their city operations without prejudice. CRPE has assembled a Portfolio School District Network of 38 cities and counties (see box below) that aspire to make their district not just the operator of its own schools but also a fair overseer of a "portfo-

Districts exploring a "School Portfolio" approach...	
Austin	Jefferson Parish, Louisiana
Baltimore	Lawrence, Massachusetts
Boston	Los Angeles
Bridgeport	Memphis
Central Falls, Rhode Island	Minneapolis
Chicago	Nashville
Cincinnati	New Haven
Clark County, Nevada	New London
Cleveland	New Orleans
Columbus, Ohio	New York City
Denver	Oakland
Detroit	Philadelphia
District of Columbia	Reynoldsburg, Ohio
Fullerton, California	Sacramento
Fulton County, Georgia	St. Louis
Hartford	Spokane
Henry County, Georgia	Spring Branch, Texas
Houston	Tennessee Achievement Schl. Dist.
Indianapolis	Windham, Connecticut

...And the Seven Principles they are asked to pursue
School choices for all families Options for families are the necessary starting place. To make this possible, districts should come up with systems for allowing children to be enrolled in the schools which fit them best in the judgement of their family. New school operators should be recruited to expand choices.
School autonomy Because the most important figure in improving student achievement is the school leader, principals and other school managers should be given as much authority as possible to hire and fire teachers and staff, control budgets, choose curricula, and buy services. In exchange, school leaders must be held accountable for results.
Pupil-based funding Money allotted for education should follow the student wherever he or she goes. Schools of different types will be entitled to the same payments for a given successful outcome.
Finding new school talent . Alternative pipelines should be used to find teachers and principals. Empirical evaluation systems should be employed to reward or remove teachers based on student outcomes. Schools are freed to pay and lay off based on performance rather than seniority.
Operational independence Schools are free to seek support from philanthropists and other funders beyond the district office. They are free to seek out their own vendors, regardless of established district patterns or contracts. New approaches and new technology are welcomed.
Performance-based accountability A clear and common framework for measuring results is put in place, and results are made public every year. Accountability is focused on student performance and improvement. Effective educators are rewarded, effective schools are replicated, struggling schools receive extra assistance, and chronically low-performing schools are closed.
Openness and public engagement Portfolio district leaders need strong public engagement and open sharing of information to build the support needed to weather the large-scale change and upheaval that entrenched interests will experience as this strategy is implemented.

Source: Adapted from guidelines by the Center on Reinventing Public Education at the University of Washington

lio" of schools operated by others within district boundaries. Network members meet twice a year. The aim is that the district bureaucracy will gradually shift toward aiding all schools, and holding every one, of whatever structure, accountable for high-quality outcomes, closing down and replacing those that don't produce good results for their students.

Districts are asked to pay attention to what works, and what doesn't, and to let go of many of the details of school operations, leaving these to be decided by leaders within the schools themselves. The seven principles that CRPE asks participating school districts to follow in a portfolio strategy are spelled out on page 145. The principles are politically ambitious, but well founded in research on school effectiveness.

This portfolio philosophy represents a kind of charter school ethic writ large across an entire school district's operations. Families get options. Principals and teachers get the freedom to organize their schools as they think best. Independent operators of schools are recruited. Fresh pipelines for teacher talent are opened and performance-based pay is inaugurated. Funding follows the child. Schools are held accountable for measurable outcomes. The emphasis is on serving students, not protecting existing institutions and adult employees.

If actually put into effect, the portfolio strategy would enact a cessation of hostilities between school districts and charter schools that have historically had such rocky relationships. Resources and responsibilities would be shared among all types of schools, with those that produce the best outcomes for their pupils gradually replacing others. Charter schools located in portfolio districts are supposed to be given more equitable funding, access to facilities, help with back-office functions like payroll and health-insurance administration. The biggest winners are parents and students, who benefit from a more diverse supply of schools and higher and more consistent standards.

Obviously this will require any sincere school district to completely reinvent its central office structures so that charter schools can become a normal part of serving students. So far, some of the participating localities (like Denver) have gone much deeper than others. This work is heavily supported by the Michael & Susan Dell Foundation, which has invested both money and staffing in districts that have signed on.

Several of the school districts experimenting with CRPE's portfolio strategy are doing so at the behest of a city mayor who controls the local schools, or some other local political leader. Unfortunately, a city's commitment to the seven principles can vanish overnight when a new politician is elected. It is unlikely, for instance, that New York City will remain a leader of the portfolio approach now that the transition from the Bloomberg to the de Blasio administration has taken place.

Operating "portfolio" school districts in real life

In an interesting philanthropically funded experiment, the state of Tennessee is using the portfolio-district approach to attack some of its most difficult educational problems. Redefining what it means to be a district, the Tennessee Achievement School District pulls together schools from across the state that are rated in the bottom 5 percent by achievement. It gives these underperformers their own transformed marching orders and funding stream, under their own superintendent. And with donations from the Walton, Joyce, Hyde Family, Pyramid Peak, and Poplar foundations, along with others, this portfolio district has set a goal of moving its member schools off the bottom rung of Tennessee schools and into the top quarter.

The Walton money provided start-up grants for new charter schools to serve children in the Achievement School District. The Joyce and Hyde contributions funded the Tennessee Charter School Incubator, which will be used to attract and train high-quality candidates interested in founding the new charter schools that the ASD needs. If this attempt to bolster weak schools through a unified portfolio approach works, other portfolio districts will undoubtedly be attempted in other places. Almost certainly these will attract philanthropic support, and become laboratories for public-school reform generally.

Already the Broad Foundation is doing something similar in Michigan. Many of the lowest-performing 5 percent of schools in that state will be taken over by Michigan's new Education Achievement Authority. The effort began in 2012 when the Authority assumed operational control of 15 underachieving schools in Detroit. As schools are taken over, all teachers and administrators must reapply for their jobs; many do not return. The schools are given responsibility to remake themselves under new leaders. Many innovations from charter schools are being adopted: longer school days and school years, flexibility for classroom innovation, new curricula, decentralized control and more accountability at the school level, and so forth. The Authority aims to build "a system of autonomous schools," and cites New Orleans, "which has aggressively chartered new schools and given greater autonomy to improving schools" as a model.

In a series of influential 2012 blog postings, Neerav Kingsland urged reform-minded school-district leaders to become "relinquishers" willing to give up district authority in order to make way for more charter schools of the sort that have performed strongly in New Orleans and other cities. In most urban areas, Kingsland argued, the soundest educational reform strategy will be for school districts to end their central monopoly on operating schools and allow more charters to flourish.

In too many places, school districts continue to hinder the introduction of charter schools. Yet some district leaders (often with philanthropic backing) have recognized that chartering can play an important role in overall school improvement. Large school districts like New York City, Chicago, Philadelphia, and Denver have recently decided that instead of investing exclusively in efforts to improve conventional schools, they will also allow new charter schools to play an important role in their city.

During the Bloomberg administration, for instance, charters in New York City went from 14 schools serving 3,000 students to 159 schools serving almost 60,000 students. Mind you, another 53,000 children remain on charter school waiting lists, and New York's school authorities also opened 140,000 seats in new district-run schools, so they hardly relinquished their role as school operators. But they did allow charters to become a richer part of the city mix. In the process, they gained sharply improved student outcomes.

Where district leaders are not willing to decentralize control and share some of their authority with a new bloom of charter schools, political leaders may need to override shortsighted school officials. Experts like Andrew Smarick and the authors of the Mind Trust's report *Opportunity Schools* have called on state policymakers to push for widespread chartering and increased autonomy for neighborhood schools, even if school districts resist. Philanthropists can urge local leaders to consider the portfolio model, and their financial assistance can be decisive in helping such ventures succeed once begun.

There is a line to be carefully trod when pushing school districts to embrace chartering. It is, after all, the independence of charter schools that allows them to be unusually effective. If chartering becomes a district-led, district-controlled, politicized, or bureaucratized process, that can undermine the promise of truly independent schools.

The abortive 2012 experience in Austin, Texas, is an illustration. The Austin school district announced that a floundering school where more than 95 percent of the students are classified as economically disadvantaged would be converted into a district-run charter managed by IDEA Public Schools. IDEA is a highly successful operator of charters in southern and central Texas. But an offshoot of the Occupy Austin movement got involved and raised a ruckus with parents and the school district. After much nastiness and a political campaign that ousted three school board members, district authorities cut their ties to IDEA and turned the school back into a conventional operation.

That offers a cautionary on the risk of in-district chartering. In places, though, where leaders are committed to giving charters the freedom to run their own operations, and merely be accountable for good student results, partnerships between charters and school districts can be helpful to students and localities alike. The gifts and guidance of donors can encourage this sort of cooperation.

Menus of Possible Investments

Obstacles that have for decades prevented millions of children from having access to excellent schooling are gradually being overcome by high-quality charter schools. Charters are bringing more entrepreneurial leadership and much more innovation into education. They are entrusting classroom authority to educators who long to be professionally empowered in this way. They are fostering greater accountability for student results.

By harnessing these new approaches, high-performing charter schools are changing the life trajectories of legions of children. Parents whose zip codes once relegated their offspring to dreadful education now have options.

So how can philanthropists give this wagon an additional push? The answer will depend on your objectives, interests, region of operation, quantity of money, and tolerance for risk.

To generate ideas for donors looking to expand their giving to charter schools, or those just getting started, The Philanthropy Roundtable recently surveyed experienced individual givers, foundations, nonprofits, and education-reform leaders on funding strategies. The table that follows presents some of their recommendations for investing at different levels. We've organized the ideas by the topics focused on in each chapter of this book.

Of course, general operating support for high-quality charter schools already educating students is often the most helpful assistance of all. Donors should be careful about telling schools what they ought to be doing next. And it's important not to offer funding only for new projects that create new duties for schools. When it comes to today's high-quality charter schools, getting them to just do more of the same can be wonderfully productive.

There are options here for everyone.

Investment

	$10k-$100k	$100k-$500k	$500k+
Increasing the supply of good charters	• Fund the general operations of statewide or city charter-support organizations (e.g. the California Charter Schools Association, New Schools for New Orleans, the D.C. Association of Chartered Public Schools, etc.) • Invest in a charter incubator that identifies leaders and equips them to launch schools • Provide funds directly to some promising local group that is designing a new charter school • Offer support to a charter school that has been approved to open in your area • Offer money for an existing local charter school to increase its number of seats • Fund periodic gatherings of charter operators focused specifically on	• Fund the general operations of statewide or city charter-support organizations • Help a successful single-site school expand to an additional campus • Help an existing charter school add extra grades every year • Make a large grant to support the startup of a promising new charter school • Provide funds that let a successful charter operator meet the needs of some student group it does not yet serve well • Support successful existing charter operators as they plan expansions of their network • Partner with other funders to seed new charter schools in areas of high need where they are currently absent	• Fund the general operations of statewide or city charter-support organizations • Make a major contribution to a new charter startup, or the launch of a new school by an existing high-quality operator • Provide funds for an existing charter school to start serving a new age group (e.g. an elementary school adding a high school) • Make a multi-year commitment to fund school networks that achieve ambitious growth targets while maintaining quality • Create or contribute to a charter school incubator • Invest in the migration of one of today's star charter operators into some key geographic

	$10k-$100k	$100k-$500k	$500k+
Increasing the supply of good charters *(continued)*	encouraging rapid growth with excellence • Organize visits to charter schools by local civic leaders and fellow philanthropists who may not be aware of their achievements • Help pay for efforts by local charter schools to market themselves, and their student outcomes, to local families • Advocate on behalf of charter schools with local officials in school districts, city government, and state legislatures, including for the raising of caps on charter school numbers • Contribute annually to the groups that collect funds from many donors and then invest them in school growth or launches (e.g. the Charter School Growth Fund, NewSchool Venture Fund, etc.)	• Pay for curricula, technology, and planning costs to allow a failing school to be restarted as a new charter • Contribute annually to the groups that collect funds from many donors and then invest them in new-school launches • Work with other local donors to bring in one of the top charter operators to reproduce their successful formula in your region • Provide a loan guarantee or other help that allows a charter operator to obtain or improve a building • Help fund the creation of new high-quality authorizers	region that is new to them • Provide facility financing assistance or loan guarantees that help new schools find buildings • Fund statewide authorizers to create separate divisions that encourage districts to hand failing schools over to charter operators as "turnaround schools," or in groups as "turnaround districts" • Fund creation of an alternative school to meet the needs of specific, difficult-to-serve populations • Contribute annually to the groups that collect funds from many donors and then invest them in new-school launches • Commission and distribute readable research reports about outcomes in charter schools

	$10k-$100k	$100k-$500k	$500k+
Increasing the supply of good charters *(continued)*	• Provide money for a charter authorizer to enhance its capacity		
Improving quality and accountability	• Contribute annually to intermediary groups that collect funding from many donors and then invest it in strengthening charter schools • Fund an annual report on quality in your state's charter school sector, spotlighting problems and strengths • Support a study comparing the learning results of local charter schools with similar district schools in the community • Pay schools to adopt proven testing and assessment systems • Support development of websites that increase the availability of clear public information	• Contribute annually to intermediary groups that collect funding from many donors and then invest it in strengthening charter schools • Fund an annual report on quality in your state's charter school sector, spotlighting problems and strengths • Fund the creation of new organizations that support charter operators trying to improve failed conventional schools they have taken over from districts • Invest in statewide authorizers, including by training, recruiting, and funding strong authorizer staff • Commission reports assessing	• Contribute annually to intermediary groups that collect funding from many donors and then invest it in strengthening charter schools • Fund an effort to get new high-quality school authorizing boards created in several states • Fund a handful of authorizers in key regions to improve their systems for vetting charter applicants, including retrospective research which identifies the initial qualities possessed by applicants who later created flourishing schools • Invest in the creation of a national database of charter schools that rates the

	$10k-$100k	$100k-$500k	$500k+
Improving quality and accountability *(continued)*	on school performance • Support initiatives to improve statewide authorizing policy and practice • Hire consultants or staff for authorizers who will create improved ways to measure and evaluate the schools under their umbrellas, and otherwise improve practice • Offer authorizers administrative or other help to fuel replications of the highest-performing charters in their region • Provide support to authorizers willing to revoke charters where student outcomes remain poor even after attempts to improve the school	the performance of various authorizers • Offer authorizers administrative or other help to fuel replications of the highest-performing charters in their region • Provide support to authorizers willing to revoke charters where student outcomes remain poor even after attempts to improve the school	performance of their students so stronger charters can influence weaker peers • Fund initiatives that financially reward teachers and staff at charters that achieve excellent outcomes • Create prizes for schools that consistently produce top student results • Provide or broker social services for needy students in schools where a lack of such services is dragging down student achievement • Support case studies analyzing high-performing charters nationwide; identify and publicize lessons learned
Bringing top teachers and principals to charters	• Help local charter schools institute "value-added" systems for teacher assessment	• Help charter networks develop "value-added" systems for teacher assessment	• Help charter networks develop "value-added" systems for teacher assessment

	$10k-$100k	$100k-$500k	$500k+
Bringing top teachers and principals to charters *(continued)*	(like D.C.'s), to identify strong and weak teachers so the first can be rewarded and the second can be offered personalized help	(like D.C.'s), to identify strong and weak teachers so the first can be rewarded and the second can be offered personalized help	(like D.C.'s), to identify strong and weak teachers so the first can be rewarded and the second can be offered personalized help
	• Invest in one of the existing programs or fellowships for developing school leaders	• Provide startup funding for intermediary organizations focused on developing principals	• Found a sustainable independent hiring program that finds top-quality teacher candidates and feeds them to charter schools
	• Pay for a promising local charter leader to receive training in one of these leadership development programs	• Create or invest in an organization that identifies professionals in other fields who could be good educators, and then recruits them to change professions	• Expand into new cities one or more of the independent, new-format education schools that train teachers to work in charter schools (like Relay)
	• Underwrite school efforts to recruit high-potential teachers and principals, especially those lacking conventional credentials	• Fund development of selection tools that help identify individuals with the potential to be top teachers	• Fund existing teacher colleges that treat charters as equal destinations for graduates and train accordingly
	• Find and support promising charter leaders from minority communities	• Support a residency model for beginning teachers	• Fund high-profile tenured research positions at teacher colleges to be staffed by academics who have shown an interest in charters and a willingness to conduct fair research on them
	• Create awards to showcase and reward excellence in charter teaching and charter leadership	• Invest in one of the independent, new-format education schools (like Relay) that train teachers to	

	$10k-$100k	$100k-$500k	$500k+
Bringing top teachers and principals to charters *(continued)*	• Hold events that bring together excellent teachers from charters, district schools, and private schools, plus teacher candidates, in places where they can observe charter schools in action and learn about employment opportunities • Offer local schools help with bolstering their boards; or donate to Charter Board Partners, The High Bar, or another group which assists charters with board development	work in charter schools • Support operators who want to shift to a new staffing model that melds teachers, aides, and computerized instruction in blended learning schools • Create prizes that recognize the nation's best charter school teachers • Invest in internal training programs that help large charter networks cultivate leaders within their ranks	• Train high-performing new principals for charters • Fund pilots that offer teachers and leaders at charter schools strong pay incentives linked to positive student outcomes • Commission reports on the state and national levels proposing new methods of value-added teacher compensation, promotion, and classroom control designed to attract and keep talented individuals in the profession
Encouraging public policies that help charters flourish*	• Invest in existing local, state, and national charter advocacy organizations • Undertake studies of state laws and federal programs that may be helping or hindering advancement of quality charter growth; circulate results among legislators	• Invest in existing local, state, and national charter advocacy organizations • Fund new advocacy efforts that build support for charters in public opinion and public policy • Create groups that unite parents of charter	• Invest in organizations focused specifically on advocacy for charter schools, or training parents of charter school children to advocate for themselves • Invest in close analysis of public policies that inhibit charter

* Some of these actions are not appropriate for a 501(c)(3). See page 104.

	$10k-$100k	$100k-$500k	$500k+
Encouraging public policies that help charters flourish *(continued)*	• Commission research and drafting of model charter laws, contracts, and policies • Commission research and reports on state policies or authorizing practices in need of improvement • Support local grassroots initiatives that champion charters • Create a speaker series or fund local PR campaigns to promote awareness of charter options • Arrange for local community leaders, business people, and policymakers to visit successful charter schools and interact with their leaders, teachers, students, and families • Take a role in local or state political activities with implications for charter schools	students and help them voice their interests • Fund development of literature to educate voters on local candidates' positions on charter schools • Commission research on portfolio districts and the benefits of district/charter collaboration • Organize a campaign in your region or state to equalize per-pupil payments, whether the child is attending a charter school or a conventional school • Pay for standing outreach and publicity campaigns at successful charter schools and networks • Take a role in local or state political activities with implications for charter schools	success, publicize these barriers, and lobby for their removal • Support development of comprehensive advocacy and public relations strategies for specific cities or states • Fund a documentary film to raise public awareness and build political pressure for more good charter schools and charter-friendly laws • Endow standing outreach and publicity arms at successful charter schools and networks • Take a role in local or state political activities with implications for charter schools

	$10k-$100k	$100k-$500k	$500k+
Solving special operational issues	• Contribute to the building campaigns of promising or high-performing charter schools • In all contacts with education officials, push for fairer provisioning of facilities to charter schools • Contribute to the annual budgets of special-ed cooperatives that serve many charter schools • Help local charters recruit and train board members • Help a charter school create the IT backbone for its school	• Fund ways for smaller local charter schools to share back-office services, vendors, and personnel • Sponsor training and vendor research to improve internal operations at schools • Fund websites, data systems, assessment tests, and performance measures that can be shared by local charters • Give charters funding to find and recruit excellent CEOs, COOs, and CFOs • Create and distribute widely a program for recruiting and training board members for local charters	• Offer major support to nonprofits that provide facilities funds to charter schools • Offer below-market loans or financial guarantees that help schools acquire, construct, or renovate facilities • Make program-related investments of your foundation endowment in revolving funds the help charter schools acquire facilities • Create new support organizations or businesses that provide back-office services to charter schools • Create or fund special-ed cooperatives that serve multiple charter schools • Fund a charter operator setting up a blended learning school

INDEX

ABOUT THE PHILANTHROPY ROUNDTABLE

The Philanthropy Roundtable is America's leading network of charitable donors working to strengthen our free society, uphold donor intent, and protect the freedom to give. Our members include individual philanthropists, families, corporations, and private foundations.

Mission

The Philanthropy Roundtable's mission is to foster excellence in philanthropy, to protect philanthropic freedom, to assist donors in achieving their philanthropic intent, and to help donors advance liberty, opportunity, and personal responsibility in America and abroad.

Principles

- Philanthropic freedom is essential to a free society
- A vibrant private sector generates the wealth that makes philanthropy possible
- Voluntary private action offers solutions to many of society's most pressing challenges
- Excellence in philanthropy is measured by results, not by good intentions
- A respect for donor intent is essential to long-term philanthropic success

Services

World-class conferences

The Philanthropy Roundtable connects you with other savvy donors. Held across the nation throughout the year, our meetings assemble grantmakers and experts to develop strategies for excellent local, state, and national giving. You will hear from innovators in K–12 education, economic opportunity, higher education, national security, and other fields. Our Annual Meeting is the Roundtable's flagship event, gathering the nation's most public-spirited and influential philanthropists for debates, how-to sessions, and discussions on the best ways for private individuals to achieve powerful results through their giving. The Annual Meeting is a stimulating and enjoyable way to meet principled donors seeking the breakthroughs that can solve our nation's greatest challenges.

Breakthrough groups

Our Breakthrough groups—focused program areas—build a critical mass of donors around a topic where dramatic results are within reach. Breakthrough groups become a springboard to help donors achieve lasting effects from their philanthropy. Our specialized staff of experts helps grantmakers invest with care. The Roundtable's K–12 education program is our largest and longest-running Breakthrough group. This network helps donors zero in on today's most promising school reforms. We are the industry-leading convener for philanthropists seeking systemic improvements through competition and parental choice, administrative freedom and accountability, student-centered technology, enhanced teaching and school leadership, and high standards and expectations for students of all backgrounds. We foster productive collaboration among donors of varied ideological perspectives who are united by a devotion to educational excellence.

A powerful voice

The Roundtable's public-policy project, the Alliance for Charitable Reform (ACR), works to advance the principles and preserve the rights of private giving. ACR educates legislators and policymakers about the central role of charitable giving in American life and the crucial importance of protecting philanthropic freedom—the ability of individuals and private organizations to determine how and where to direct their charitable assets. Active in Washington, D.C., and in the states, ACR protects charitable giving, defends the diversity of charitable causes, and battles intrusive government regulation. We believe the capacity of private initiative to address national problems must not be burdened with costly or crippling constraints.

Protection of donor interests

The Philanthropy Roundtable is the leading force in American philanthropy to protect donor intent. Generous givers want assurance that their money will be used for the specific charitable aims and purposes they believe in, not redirected to some other agenda. Unfortunately, donor intent is usually violated in increments, as foundation staff and trustees neglect or misconstrue the founder's values and drift into other purposes. Through education, practical guidance, legislative action, and individual consultation, The Philanthropy Roundtable is active in guarding donor intent. We are happy to advise you on steps you can take to ensure that your mission and goals are protected.

Must-read publications
Philanthropy, the Roundtable's quarterly magazine, is packed with useful and beautifully written real-life stories. It offers practical examples, inspiration, detailed information, history, and clear guidance on the differences between giving that is great and giving that disappoints. We also publish a series of guidebooks that provide detailed information on the very best ways to be effective in particular aspects of philanthropy. These guidebooks are compact, brisk, and readable. Most focus on one particular area of giving—for instance, Catholic schools, support for veterans, anti-poverty programs, technology in education. Real-life examples, hard numbers, the experiences of other donors, recent history, and policy guidance are presented to inform and inspire savvy donors.

Join the Roundtable!
When working with The Philanthropy Roundtable, members are better equipped to achieve long-lasting success with their charitable giving. Your membership in the Roundtable will make you part of a potent network that understands philanthropy and strengthens our free society. Philanthropy Roundtable members range from Forbes 400 individual givers and the largest American foundations to small family foundations and donors just beginning their charitable careers. Our members include:

- Individuals and families
- Private foundations
- Community foundations
- Venture philanthropists
- Corporate giving programs
- Large operating foundations and charities that devote more than half of their budget to external grants

Philanthropists who contribute at least $100,000 annually to charitable causes are eligible to become members of the Roundtable and register for most of our programs. Roundtable events provide you with a solicitation-free environment.

For more information on The Philanthropy Roundtable or to learn about our individual program areas, please call (202) 822-8333 or e-mail main@PhilanthropyRoundtable.org.

ABOUT THE AUTHOR

Karl Zinsmeister is editor of The Philanthropy Roundtable's guidebook series, which include volumes on blended learning, high-achieving students, teacher and principal excellence, charter schools, Catholic schools, and other topics of interest to education donors, as well as books on philanthropy for the poor, veterans and military families, and other causes. He also oversees *Philanthropy* magazine, and the Roundtable's website and online publications. He is creating the forthcoming *Almanac of American Philanthropy*. Zinsmeister has authored eight books, made a PBS film, and written hundreds of articles for publications ranging from *The Atlantic* to the *Wall Street Journal* to *Reader's Digest*. He previously was a Senate aide to Daniel Patrick Moynihan, the J. B. Fuqua Fellow at the American Enterprise Institute, and Director of the White House Domestic Policy Council and chief domestic policy adviser to President George W. Bush. He is a graduate of Yale University and also studied at Trinity College Dublin.